ॐ

SANSKRIT GRAMMAR
Playful Enquiry

Ashwini Kumar Aggarwal

जय गुरुदेव

ISBN13: 978-81-944890-0-9 Paperback Edition
ISBN13: 978-81-944890-1-6 Hardbound Edition
ISBN13: 978-81-944890-2-3 Digital Edition

Title: Sanskrit Grammar Playful Enquiry

Printed and Published by
Devotees of Sri Sri Ravi Shankar Ashram
34 Sunny Enclave, Devigarh Road,
Patiala 147001, Punjab, India

https://advaita56.weebly.com/
The Art of Living Centre

https://www.artofliving.org/

7th January 2020 Dvadashi Tithi
Krittika Nakshatra, Shukla Paksha, Pausha Masa, Dakshinayana
Vikram Samvat 2076 Paridhavi, Saka Era 1941 Vikari

1st Edition January 2020

जय गुरुदेव

Dedication

Gurudev Sri Sri Ravi Shankar

We need the help of language to understand what we are
worrying or not worrying about.

An offering at His Lotus feet

Acknowledgements
A great shift to a new workplace, home, and Ashram on Gurpurab,
the 550th anniversary of Guru Nanak, Nov 2019.

Cover Photo Credits
https://pixabay.com/photos/child-colors-nepal-india-finger-3194977/
Image by Prashant Sharma from Pixabay.

जय गुरुदेव

Preface

Having spent some years in the enquiry of Sanskrit, its literature and epics, and its Vyakarana. Having spent many fruitful moments of teaching and interacting with bright youngsters.

We here present some of our experiences in the Enquiry of this worth knowing Language. With a happy playful child-like simplicity.

May you enjoy Sanskrit as much as we do.
May your study be supremely rewarding.
May your vision expand and life take a beautiful turn.

ॐ तत् सत् । Om Tat Sat.

Blessing

ज्ञानाधिष्ठानं मातृका । १.४

Carefully observe and distinguish the different ideas, thoughts or worries that arise in your mind. Then observe one thought, then one sentence and then one word. Then separate that one word into letters and look at each letter carefully. When you do this, your worries will disappear.

Practice this for one week and you will understand that when we hold onto the silence that is in between words, then worries vanish.

A mantra, a sacred sound, is defined as "मननात् त्रायते इति मन्त्रः" A mantra is that, which when repeated constantly clears your mind from worries and protects you.

Knowledge is bondage, and it is impossible to gain knowledge without words. We need the help of language to understand what we are worrying or not worrying about. When we separate the words, we will be free from worry.

H H Sri Sri Ravi Shankar
an excerpt from commentary on the Shiva Sutras

Table of Contents

Introduction

The Sanskrit Alphabet वर्णमाला consists of 56 letters.

- Vowels स्वर - 20 (popular tradition lists 13, without pluta)
- Consonants व्यञ्जन - 34 (popular tradition lists 33, without ळ)
- Anusvara and visarga – 2 (the ayogavahas).

Consonant and Halant
- A written consonant क is usually supplied with the vowel अ for purpose of enunciation.
- Without vowel, a हलन्त symbol is used to write a consonant. Actual consonant should be with a halant, i.e. क् ।
- The ह is an aspirate, i.e. mahaprana. It is named thus.

Anusvara and Candrabindu
- An anusvara ◌ं is a nasal नासिका , uttered with mouth closed and emphasis on the nose. usually pronounced as म्
- The candrabindu ◌ँ is an anunasika अनुनासिका , uttered from the mouth with emphasis on the nose.

Visarga, Jihvamuliya and Upadhmaniya
- Visarga ◌: is a very special letter that is enunciated in various ways depending upon its placement
- Jihvamuliya ✕ is a guttural visarga seen in Vedic texts
- Upadhmaniya ✕ (ꣽ) is a labial visarga seen in Vedic texts

Avagraha ऽ denotes the elision of अ to prevent loss of meaning.
ळ is usually found in Vedic texts and rarely in classical Sanskrit.

Sanskrit numerals combine like the English numerals when written, units, tens, thousands, e.g. 1 = १, 10 = १०, 100 = १००, 1568 = १५६८

The Sanskrit Alphabet संस्कृत वर्णमाला

Sanskrit संस्कृत is written in the देवनागरी Devanagari script, whereas English is written in the Roman script. Popular tradition lists it as

अ आ इ ई उ ऊ ऋ ॠ ऌ ॡ   ए ऐ ओ औ   अं अः   ॐ

क	ख	ग	घ	ङ	The Shiva Sounds
च	छ	ज	झ	ञ	
ट	ठ	ड	ढ	ण	The Brahma Sounds
त	थ	द	ध	न	
प	फ	ब	भ	म	The Vishnu Sounds
य र ल व		श ष स		ह	
		ळ		व्ह	Vedic Sanskrit
० १ २ ३ ४ ५ ६ ७ ८ ९					Numerals
क्ष ज्ञ श्र					Conjunct letter
Consonants written with the vowel अ for enunciation					

The vowel long ॡ is not found in literature. It is given only in grammar books or in font sets. Hence crossed out.

Letter variations in Sanskrit texts

अ = ॲ , आ = ॳ , ओ = ॴ , औ = ॵ , झ = झ़ , ण = रा

Conjunct letter संयुक्त अक्षर

क्ष , ज्ञ , श्र are not letters of the alphabet. Rather these are conjuncts that have become popular in writing. An earlier form of क्ष is क्त ।

Alphabet as Commonly Written

The Sanskrit alphabet is commonly written without a halant. Consonants cannot be uttered without a vowel. So in teaching, each consonant is supplied with the vowel अ , so that it can be uttered. Here are the 56 letters of the classical Sanskrit Alphabet.

20 Vowels (ह्रस्वः , दीर्घः , प्लुतः)

अ आ अ३ इ ई इ३ उ ऊ उ३ ऋ ॠ ऋ३ ऌ ऌ३ ए ऐ ए३ ओ औ ओ३

34 Consonants

क ख ग घ ङ

च छ ज झ ञ

ट ठ ड ढ ण

त थ द ध न

प फ ब भ म

य र ल व श ष स ह and ळ

2 Ayogavahas अं अः

Maheshwar Sutras माहेश्वराणि सूत्राणि

Encompasses sounds that are the foundation of the Devanagari Alphabet. Attributed to Maharishi Panini circa 600 BC.

1	अ इ उ	ण्	All vowels = अ च् letters
2	ऋ ऌ	क्	Simple vowels = अ क् letters
3	ए ओ	ङ्	Diphthongs = ए च् letters
4	ऐ औ	च्	Semivowels = य ण् letters
Vowel – Consonant boundary			
5	ह य व र	ट्	All consonants = ह ल् letters
6	लँ	ण्	=ल्+अँ, No nasal equiv. for र्
7	ञ म ङ ण न	म्	5th of row = Nasals = ञ म् letters
8	झ भ	ञ्	4th of row = झ ष् letters
9	घ ढ ध	ष्	are all soft consonants
10	ज ब ग ड द	श्	3rd of row = ज श् letters (soft)
11	ख फ छ ठ थँ च ट त	व्	1st and 2nd of row = ख य् letters
12	क प	य्	are all hard consonants
13	श ष स	र्	Sibilants (hard) = श र् letters
14	ह	ल्	Aspirate is soft

Vowel Symbols and Attaching to Consonants

Whenever in a word, vowels follow consonants, they get attached to them and a new symbol gets written.

Consider the template matrix

Final Glyph	Vowel Signs	Exceptions
क् + अ = क	ॖ + अ	
क् + आ = का	ा	
क् + इ = कि	ि	
क् + ई = की	ी	
क् + उ = कु	ु	र् + उ = रु (not र्‍)
क् + ऊ = कू	ू	र् + ऊ = रू
क् + ऋ = कृ	ृ	ह् + ऋ = हृ
क् + ॠ = कॄ	ॄ	
क् + ऌ = कॢ	ॢ	
क् + ए = के	े	
क् + ऐ = कै	ै	
क् + ओ = को	ो	
क् + औ = कौ	ौ	
क् + अं = कं	ं , ँ	
क् + अः = कः	ः	

Similarly two or more consonants following each other in a word are written as new symbols, e.g. क् + र् + अ = क्र । र् + क् + अ = र्क ।

Writing and Identifying the Devanagari Letters

Devanagari letters are written with a top horizontal bar. In the Indian tradition, having a cap, pagri, tilak or such ornamentation is considered auspicious.

अ is like a "3" attached to a "T" i.e. 3-T

आ is like a "3-I" with a "T" i.e. 3-IT

इ is like an "S" with a tail.

ई is like an "S" with a tail and a furl.

उ is like an exaggerated "3".

ऊ is like an exaggerated "3" with a tail.

ए is like a "P" with a slant.

ऐ is like a "P" with a slant and a grave accent.

ओ is like "3-IT" with a grave accent.

औ is like "3-IT" with two grave accents.

The Visarga is like a colon = ◌ः

The Anusvara is like the dot above " i " = ◌ं

The Full stop at end of a sentence is like the vertical bar = ।

The Full stop at end of a paragraph is like two vertical bars = ॥

A Word beginning with each letter of the alphabet

अ अक्षरं letter	आ आत्मा soul	इ इन्द्रः Indra	ई ईश्वरः Lord
उ उष्ट्रः camel	ऊ ऊर्णम् wool	ऋ ऋग्वेदः Rigveda	ॠ ॠणाति moves
ऌ ऌकारः letter ऌ	ए एकं one	ऐ ऐरावतः Elephant	ओ ओषधिः herb
औ औपवास्यं fast	अं अंबरं sky	अः Ahh	ळ ळकारः letter ळ

क कन्या virgin	ख खगः bird	ग गुरुः master	घ घटी clock	ङ ङकारः Letter ङ
च चमसः spoon	छ छत्रम् umbrella	ज जलम् water	झ झटिति quickly	ञ अकारः Letter ञ
ट टंकः axe	ठ ठक्कुरः idol	ड डमरुः drum	ढ ढालं shield	ण णकारः Letter ण
त तरुणः boy	थ थूत्कारः spitting sound	द दुग्धं milk	ध धेनुः cow	न नदी river
प पिता father	फ फलं fruit	ब बकः heron	भ भगिनी sister	म माता mother
य युवती girl	र राजा king	ल लता creeper	व वधूः bride	
श शिला rock	ष षोडश sixteen	स सर्पः snake	ह हंसः swan	

Commonly used Words

मम mine नमस्ते hello	भवतः yours (to a gentleman)	भवत्याः yours (to a lady)	आवश्यकम् necessary
सः he	सा she	तत् it	पर्याप्तम् okay
एषः this (mas)	एषा this (fem)	एतत् this (neu)	अभ्यासः lesson
स्वीकरोतु please accept	भवान् you (to a man respectfully	भवती you (to a woman respectfully	त्वम् you (general use)
आम् yes	न no	मास्तु do not	परिचयः intro
अस्ति it is	नास्ति it is not	सर्वत्र everywhere	एकत्र only one
अत्र here	तत्र there	अन्यत्र elsewhere	आरभ्य since
पुरतः in front of	पृष्ठतः behind	वामतः to left of	दक्षिणतः to right

उपरि above	अधः below	अन्तः till end	रिक्तस्थानं blank
स्वागतम् welcome	अहम् I	धन्यवादः thanks	सुन्दरं beautiful
समीचीनम् good	सम्यक् fair	उत्तमं excellent	यत् which
कुत्र where	कदा when	कः who	किम् what
कति how many	कुतः from where	कथम् how come	किमर्थम् why
अद्य today	ह्यः yesterday	श्वः tomorrow	परश्वः day after
अद्यतन today's	ह्यस्तन yesterday's	श्वस्तन tomorrow's	पूर्वतन earlier's
तः from this time	पर्यन्तम् to that time	उच्चैः loudly	शनैः softly
कार्यम् work	विचारं thought	विषयम् topic	इत्यादि etc.
किन्तु but	निश्चयेन surely	प्रायशः generally	अपेक्षया wrt
अतः hence	यतः because	अनुवादं translation	सम्भाषणं lecture
परिशिष्टं appendix	सङ्गणकम् computer	विमानम् airplane	दूरदर्शनं television

Everyday Sentences

Hello Sister! Meet brother who arrived from America yesterday.
भोः भगिनी ! मेलनं भ्रातरम् करोसि , यः अमेरिकायाः ह्यः आगतवान् ।

How nice! Pleased to meet you Bro. अहो भाग्यम् ! मुदितोऽस्मि अनुज ।

Painting is a good hobby. चित्रकर्मं समीचीनं कलाम् अस्ति ।

Hello! Who is speaking? भोः , कः सम्भाषणं करोति ।
I am Ashwin speaking. अहम् अश्विनः वदामि ।
Would you please give her a message. कृपया ताम् एकं सन्देशं सूचयति
किम् । Sure wait a moment. आम् एकं क्षणं तिष्ठतु ।

No problem dear. भवतु चिन्तां न करोतु ।

What is the time? कः समयः ।

Pronunciation of Sanskrit Letters

उच्चारणम्

अ son आ father इ it ई beat उ full ऊ pool ऋ rhythm

ॠ marine ऌ revelry ए play ऐ aisle ओ go औ loud

अं Anusvara is pure nasal – close the lips – similar to म्

अः Visarga is Breath release like ह् and preceding vowel sound

E.g. pronounce नमः as नमह , शान्तिः as शान्तिहि , विष्णुः as विष्णुहु

क seeK	ख Khan	ग Get	घ loGHut	ङ sing
च Chunk	छ catchhim	ज Jump	झ heDGEhog	ञ bunch
ट True	ठ anTHill	ड Drum	ढ goDHead	ण under
त Tamil	थ Thunder	द That	ध breaTHE	न nut
प Put	फ Fruit	ब Bin	भ abhor	म much

य loYal र Red ल Luck व Vase श Sure ष Shun स So Hum ह

Conjuncts in general – first utter the top part and then the bottom one, e.g.

Bhagavad Gita 10.16 तिष्ठसि -> ष् ठ ,

Bhagavad Gita 10.23 शङ्करश्चास्मि -> ङ् क , श् च

Specific Conjuncts

ह् ण = ह्ण , ह् न = ह्न , ह् म = ह्म

Utter with emphasis on the chest, first the nasal and then the aspiration, e.g. Brahma = ब्रह्म *Pronounce as **Bramha***

Place & Effort of Enunciation

| Place of speech | Vowels स्वर | | Row Consonants व्यञ्जन | | | | | Semi vowel | Sibilant |
| | | | Alpaprana | | Mahaprana | | | | |
	Short	Long	1st	2nd	3rd	4th	5th	el	
कण्ठ	अ	आ	क	ख	ग	घ	ङ		
तालु	इ	ई	च	छ	ज	झ	ञ	य	श
मूर्धा	ऋ	ॠ	ट	ठ	ड	ढ	ण	र	ष
दन्त	ऌ		त	थ	द	ध	न	ल	स
ओष्ठ	उ	ऊ	प	फ	ब	भ	म		
Consonants are supplied with vowel अ to aid enunciation									

कण्ठ – तालु	ए	ऐ	Diphthongs have twin places of utterance, being compound vowels
कण्ठ – ओष्ठ	ओ	औ	
दन्त – ओष्ठ	व		The vakara is different from the other semivowels as it has twin places of utterance
नासिक्य	ֹं , अं		Anusvara is a pure Nasal
अनुनासिका	ֽँ , ॐ , यँ		Candrabindu means Nasalization

कण्ठ Soft, Mahaprana	ह	Hakara is an Aspirate. It is sounded like a soft release of breath
	०ः	Visarga is an Aspirate. It is sounded like ह along with its preceding vowel
Ardha Visarga ०ः is also written as ✕		
Base of tongue Hard, Alpaprana	०ः or ✕	Jihvamuliya pronounce as हॖ (a visarga preceding क , ख)
ओष्ठ Hard, Alpaprana or ॐ	०ः or ✕	Upadhmaniya pronounce as फॖ (a visarga preceding प , फ)

कण्ठ्य Guttural or Velar	तालव्य Palatal	मूर्धन्य Cerebral or Retroflex or Lingual	दन्त्य Dental	ओष्ठ्य Labial

All vowels and semi vowels are termed voiced घोष वर्ण । This means that a background sound is produced from the tremor in the vocal cords in addition to the active sound produced in speaking. The 3rd, 4th and 5th letters of the row class consonants are also घोष वर्ण ।

The 1st and 2nd letters of the row class consonants, the sibilants and the aspirate are termed अघोष वर्ण । This means that no background sound arises from the tremor in the vocal cords.

All row consonants are termed स्पर्श वर्ण । Tongue makes contact.

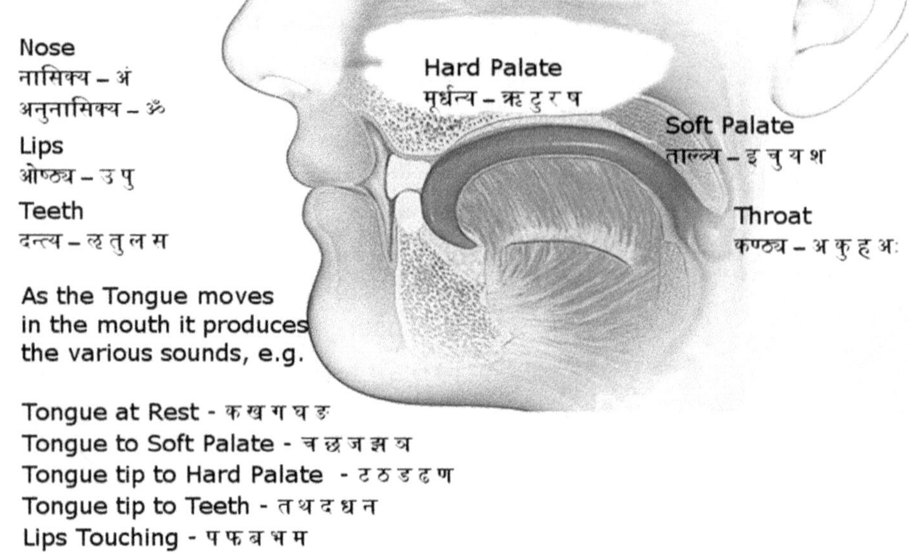

As the Tongue moves in the mouth it produces the various sounds, e.g.

Tongue at Rest - क ख ग घ ङ
Tongue to Soft Palate - च छ ज झ ञ
Tongue tip to Hard Palate - ट ठ ड ढ ण
Tongue tip to Teeth - त थ द ध न
Lips Touching - प फ ब भ म

Also the sounds reverberate in different parts within the Body and the effect of enunciating the letters is felt there, or we can say one organ or the other is connected to each sound of the alphabet.

The unit of time for enunciation is a short vowel, having 1 mātra. The long vowels and diphthongs have 2 matras. A consonant has only ½ matra and it is supplied with a vowel for proper enunciation.

VOWELS स्वर - Long Vowels are sounded twice as long as the short vowels. DIPHTHONGS सन्ध्यक्षर (सन्धि – अक्षर) Are combinations of two vowels and are sounded long.
GUTTURALS कण्ठ्य (also known as VELAR) Sounded from the throat with the tongue resting. PALATALS तालव्य (soft palate) Sounded with the tongue raised slightly. CEREBRALS मूर्धन्य (also RETROFLEX or LINGUAL, hard palate) Sounded with the tongue touching the roof of the mouth. DENTALS दन्त्य - Sounded with tongue distinctly touching the teeth. LABIALS ओष्ठ्य -Sounded with lips distinctly touching each other.

Traditional Prayers

Honoring the Master = Guru Vandana

गुरुर् ब्रह्मा गुरुर् विष्णुः , गुरुर् देवो महेश्वरः ।

गुरुस् साक्षात् परं ब्रह्म , तस्मै श्रीगुरवे नमः ॥

gurur brahmā gurur viṣṇuḥ , gurur devo maheśvaraḥ |

gurus sākṣāt paraṃ brahma , tasmai śrīgurave namaḥ ||

Obstacle Prevention = Ganesh Vandana

वक्रतुण्ड महाकाय सूर्यकोटिसमप्रभ । निर्विघ्नं कुरु मे देव सर्वकार्येषु सर्वदा ॥

vakratuṇḍa mahākāya sūryakoṭisamaprabha |
nirvighnaṃ kuru me deva sarvakāryeṣu sarvadā ||

Proper Study and Schooling = Saraswati Prarthana

सरस्वति नमस्तुभ्यं वरदे कामरूपिणि ।

विद्यारम्भं करिष्यामि सिद्धिर् भवतु मे सदा ॥

sarasvati namastubhyaṃ varade kāmarūpiṇi |
vidyārambhaṃ kariṣyāmi siddhir bhavatu me sadā ||

Keeping the Boss Happy = Vishnu Shloka

शुक्लाम्बरधरं विष्णुं शशिवर्णं चतुर्भुजम् । प्रसन्नवदनं ध्यायेत् सर्वविघ्नोपशान्तयेः ॥

śuklāmbaradharaṃ viṣṇum śaśivarṇam caturbhujam |
prasannavadanaṃ dhyāyet sarvavighnopaśāntayeḥ ||

Honoring the Five Elements = The Ultimate Divine Shiva

ॐ नमः शिवाय । oṃ namaḥ śivāya |

Honoring the Divine Mother = Devi Shloka

सर्व–मङ्गल–माङ्गल्ये , शिवे सर्वार्थ–साधिके ।

शरण्ये त्र्यम्बके गौरि , नारायणि नमोऽस्तु ते ॥

sarva–maṅgala–māṅgalye , śive sarvārtha–sādhike |

śaraṇye tryambake gauri , nārāyaṇi namo'stu te ||

Gayatri Mantra = Keeping the Intellect pure and available
ॐ भूर् भुवस् सुवः । तत् सवितुर् वरेण्यं भर्गो देवस्य धीमहि । धियो यो नः प्रचोदयात् ॥
oṃ bhūr bhuvas suvaḥ | tat savitur vareṇyaṃ bhargo devasya dhīmahi | dhiyo yo naḥ pracodayāt ||

Maha Mrityunjaye Mantra = Preventing and Overcoming Grief
ॐ त्र्यम्बकं यजामहे , सुगन्धिं पुष्टिवर्धनम् ।
उर्वारुकमिव बन्धनान् , मृत्योर् मुक्षीय माऽमृतात् ॥
oṃ tryambakaṃ yajāmahe sugandhiṃ puṣṭivardhanam |
urvārukamiva bandhanān mṛtyor mukṣīya mā'mṛtāt ||

Upanishad Peace Invocation = Group Activity or Mealtime Prayer
ॐ सह नाववतु । सह नौ भुनक्तु । सह वीर्यं करवावहै ।
तेजस्विनावधीतमस्तु मा विद्विषावहै ॥ ॐ शान्तिः शान्तिः शान्तिः ॥
oṃ saha nāvavatu | saha nau bhunaktu | saha vīryaṃ karavāvahai |
tejasvināvadhītamastu mā vidviṣāvahai || oṃ śāntiḥ śāntiḥ śāntiḥ ||

Bhagavad Gita = Banish all worry and help talents blossom
यदा यदा हि धर्मस्य , ग्लानिर् भवति भारत ।
अभ्युत्थानम् अधर्मस्य , तदात्मानं सृजाम्यहम् ॥ ४.७
yadā yadā hi dharmasya , glānir bhavati bhārata |
abhyutthānam adharmasya , tadātmānaṃ sṛjāmyaham || 4.7

General Blessing
सर्वे भवन्तु सुखिनः । सर्वे सन्तु निरामयाः ।
सर्वे भद्राणि पश्यन्तु । मा कश्चिद् दुःखभाग् भवेत् ॥
sarve bhavantu sukhinaḥ | sarve santu nirāmayāḥ |
sarve bhadrāṇi paśyantu | mā kaścid duḥkhabhāg bhavet ||

Traditional Wisdom

Our parents and grandparents use phrases and idioms that have a deep meaning. These can aid success by preventing mistakes.

Just as all raindrops and rivulets and streams proceed to the ocean alone, So does all prayer and worship go to the Same One God, hence be at ease, be peaceful, do not decry anyone's belief.

आकाशात् पतितं तोयं यथा गच्छति सागरम् ।

सर्वदेवनमस्कारः केशवं प्रतिगच्छति ॥

ākāśāt patitaṃ toyaṃ yathā gacchati sāgaram I

sarvadevanamaskāraḥ keśavaṃ pratigacchati II

Can anyone ever tell if breath shall function the next moment?
Wise it is to do today what you'd rather do tomorrow.

न हि कश्चित् विजानाति किं कस्य श्वो भविष्यति ।

अतः श्वः करणीयानि कुर्यादद्यैव बुद्धिमान् ॥

na hi kaścit vijānāti kiṃ kasya śvo bhaviṣyati I

ataḥ śvaḥ karaṇīyāni kuryādadyaiva buddhimān II

What pleasure doth thee seek that Dispassion cannot deliver?
My friend, forsake feverish covetousness, live simply, guilt-free,
within your means.

सुरमंदिरतरुमूलनिवासः शय्या भूतलमजिनं वासः ।

सर्वपरिग्रहभोगत्यागः कस्य सुखं न करोति विरागः ॥

suramaṃdiratarumūlanivāsaḥ śayyā bhūtalamajinaṃ vāsaḥ I

sarvaparigrahabhogatyāgaḥ kasya sukhaṃ na karoti virāgaḥ II

Goodness alone is Real and Everlasting, falsehood is a temporary mirage. Identify yourself with the great goodness, live the sacred principles, this is the wisdom of the scriptures.

ब्रह्म सत्यं जगन् मिथ्या , जीवो ब्रह्मैव नापरः ।

अनेन वेद्यं सच्–छास्त्रम् , इति वेदान्त–डिण्डिमः ॥

brahma satyaṃ jagan mithyā , jīvo brahmaiva nāparaḥ I

anena vedyaṃ sac–chāstram , iti vedānta–ḍiṇḍimaḥ II

These isn't ever a need to bribe or fix the results. Your merit, talent, and honest hard effort shall always get its just due; know it as the inviolable law of this karmic plane. (famous as Newton's third law). Let go of imaginary fancies, nor be attached to petty cravings.

कर्मण्येवाधिकारस्ते , मा फलेषु कदाचन ।
मा कर्मफलहेतुर् भूः , मा ते सङ्गोऽस्त्वकर्मणि ॥

karmaṇyevādhikāraste , mā phaleṣu kadācana ।
mā karmaphalahetur bhūḥ , mā te saṅgo'stvakarmaṇi ॥

Waking Up Affirmation = Honoring the Divine in every Effort

कराग्रे वसते लक्ष्मीः , कर–मध्ये सरस्वती । कर–मूले तु गोविन्दः , प्रभाते करदर्शनम् ॥

karāgre vasate lakṣmīḥ , kara–madhye sarasvatī ।
kara–mūle tu govindaḥ , prabhāte karadarśanam ॥

Traditional Thought Provoking Riddles

प्रहेलिका Guess it???
अस्थि नास्ति , शिरो नास्ति , बाहुर् अस्ति निर् अङ्गुलिः ।
नास्ति पाद–द्वयं , गाढम् अङ्गम् आलिङ्गति स्वयम् ॥
Bones none, Head none, Arm yes, without Finger.
No Feet-two, tightly body hugging self. ॥ Answer युतकम् Shirt.

A Story from the Panchatantra Tradition

चतुरः काकः The clever crow/The thirsty crow - Once upon a time एकः काकः अस्ति । one crow is. सः बहु तृषितः । He very thirsty. सः जलार्थं भ्रमति । He for-water's-sake roams. तदा ग्रीष्मकालः । Then summer-season. कुत्रापि जलं नास्ति । Anywhere water not-there. काकः कष्टेन बहुदूरं गच्छति । Crow with-effort very-far travels. तत्र सः एकं घटं पश्यति । There he a pot sees. काकस्य अतीव सन्तोषः भवति । For-crow much delight arises. किन्तु घटे स्वल्पम् एव जलम् अस्ति । However in-pot quite-little only water is. जलं कथं पिबामि water how i-drink, इति काकः चिन्तयति । thus crow broods. सः एकम् उपायं करोति । He a plan makes. शिलाखण्डान् आनयति । Rock-pieces fetches. घटे पूरयति । In-pot puts. जलम् उपरि आगच्छति । Water upwards comes. काकः सन्तोषेण जलं पिबति । Crow with-satisfaction water drinks. ततः गच्छति । Then flies.

Sutra Vartika Bhashya Vritti Prakriya

The system of Sanskrit Grammar as we learn today is founded on a hoary tradition by language experts and visionaries of the highest order. In this tradition we name some of the ancient Seers and also the contemporary grammarians.

- Sutras सूत्र are crisp Sanskrit statements that explain the Sanskrit grammar in totality by Maharshi Panini circa 6BC.
- Vartikas वार्तिक are Sanskrit statements by Katyayana circa 4BC, that edit certain Sutras or give additional information for some of the Sutras.
- Mahābhāṣya महाभाष्यम् is a voluminous Sanskrit text that elaborates some Sutras and gives succinct commentary by Maharshi Patanjali circa 2BC.
- Kāśikā Vṛttī काशिका वृत्तिः is a sutra by sutra Sanskrit explanation of all Sutras by scholars Jayaditya and Vamana circa 700AD.
- Siddhanta Kaumudi सिद्धान्त कौमुदी is a Sanskrit topic wise rearrangement of all the sutras by Bhattoji Dikshit circa 1700AD, and an oft studied text in recent times.
- Laghu Siddhanta Kaumudi by James Ballantyne written in 1840s is an English translation and topic wise commentary.
- The Ashtadhyayi of Panini by S. C. Vasu written in the 1890s is the authoritative English translation and commentary on the original Sanskrit Sutras of Panini.
- Bhaimī Vyakhya भैमी व्याख्या in Hindi is an easily understandable shortened grammar text culled from the Siddhanta Kaumudi by Bhimsen Shastri in 1950s.
- Ashtadhyayi Sahaj Bodha अष्टाध्यायी सहजबोध in Hindi by Pushpa Dikshit is the definitive guide to understanding Sanskrit grammar, a Hindi translation, section wise arrangement and explanation of the original grammar text, published in 1999.
- Prathma Vritti प्रथमावृत्ति in Hindi by Brahmadutt Jignasu is a fundamental text that covers all original Sanskrit Sutras of Panini in sequence, and is a marvelous commentary, published in 2002.

Parsing

Now begins our enquiry into the grammar of the Language. How shall we begin? What shall we attempt first?

Let us write a simple sentence and ask, what is each word here? पद-स्वरूप-वर्णनम् How is each word grammatically defined?

मम नाम संगीता । My name is Sangeeta.

In English, a literal translation would be,
मम नाम संगीता । Of_me name Sangeeta.

Let us take it word by word.

मम = This is a Pronoun. सर्वनाम शब्दः । Its stem प्रातिपदिकम् is अस्मद् । अस्मद् ends in the letter द् । So we can say अस्मद् दकारः अन्तः शब्दः । It is valid in all the three genders, त्रिषु लिङ्गेषु , and takes identical forms. समानरूपः । In the grammar books, we shall see its definition as दकारान्तः शब्दः । This is due to compound समासः formation, words दकारः अन्तः join to make दकारान्तः । We also see it is the 6th case षष्ठी विभक्तिः , singular एकवचनम् ।

The complete grammatical definition for word **मम** = "अस्मद्" दकारान्तः शब्दः , षष्ठी विभक्तिः , एकवचनम् , त्रिषु लिङ्गेषु ।

मम नाम संगीता । My name is Sangeeta.

नाम = This is a Noun. नाम शब्दः । Its stem प्रातिपदिकम् is नामन् । नामन् ends in the letter न् । So we can say नामन् नकारान्तः शब्दः । It is valid in neuter gender, नपुंसकलिङ्गः । We also see it is the 1st case प्रथमा विभक्तिः , singular एकवचनम् ।

The complete grammatical definition for word **नाम** = "नामन्" नकारान्तः शब्दः , प्रथमा विभक्तिः , एकवचनम् , नपुंसकलिङ्गः ।

मम नाम संगीता । My name is Sangeeta.

संगीता = This is a noun. नाम शब्दः । Its stem प्रातिपदिकम् is संगीता । संगीता ends in the letter आ । So we can say संगीता आकारान्तः शब्दः । It is valid in feminine gender, स्त्रीलिङ्गः । We also see it is the 1st case प्रथमा विभक्तिः , singular एकवचनम् ।

The complete grammatical definition for word संगीता = "संगीता" आकारान्तः शब्दः , प्रथमा विभक्तिः , एकवचनम् , स्त्रीलिङ्गः ।

One more thing. The technically correct spelling is सङ्गीता , but most books list it as संगीता , and we accept the common usage. This fact regarding the Anusvara ं will be evident in many words in many places. The Anusvara in Sanskrit follows certain grammar rules, however there is wide liberty in its usage.

Another technical point. See the definition statements.
"अस्मद्" दकारान्तः शब्दः , षष्ठी विभक्तिः , एकवचनम् , त्रिषु लिङ्गेषु ।
"नामन्" नकारान्तः शब्दः , प्रथमा विभक्तिः , एकवचनम् , नपुंसकलिङ्गः ।
"संगीता" आकारान्तः शब्दः , प्रथमा विभक्तिः , एकवचनम् , स्त्रीलिङ्गः ।

The Substantive or Subject Noun in these statements is शब्दः , and the other nouns are adjectives or qualifying nouns. Technically, in Sanskrit grammar, the Adjective should follow the Substantive in gender and case and number. Or at least in case and number, if the gender is fixed. Let's analyze the definition from a grammar perspective.

Substantive विशेष्य ।
शब्दः = पुंलिङ्गः प्रथमा विभक्तिः एकवचनम् । In short शब्दः m 1/1, शब्दः$^{m1/1}$

Adjective विशेषण ।
अन्तः = पुंलिङ्गः , प्रथमा विभक्तिः , एकवचनम् । अन्तः m 1/1
The stem अन्त can be declined in *masculine* and *neuter*. Here since it is an adjective to शब्दः , it must be spelled in masculine.

Adjective विशेषण ।

विभक्तिः = स्त्रीलिङ्गः , प्रथमा विभक्तिः , एकवचनम् । विभक्तिः f 1/1

The stem विभक्ति can be declined in *feminine* only. Here since it is an adjective, it maintains its feminine attribute, and must be spelled in 1st case singular.

Adjective विशेषण ।

षष्ठी = स्त्रीलिङ्गः , प्रथमा विभक्तिः , एकवचनम् । षष्ठी f 1/1

The ordinal stem षट् can be declined in *all genders*. Here since it is an adjective to विभक्तिः, it must be spelled in its feminine attribute.

Adjective विशेषण ।

एकवचनम् = नपुंसकलिङ्गः, प्रथमा विभक्तिः , एकवचनम् । एकवचनम् n 1/1

The number stem वचन can be declined in *neuter* only. Here since it is an adjective, it maintains its neuter attribute, and must be spelled in 1st case singular.

Adjective विशेषण ।

नपुंसकलिङ्गः = पुंलिङ्गः , प्रथमा विभक्तिः , एकवचनम् । नपुंसकलिङ्गः m 1/1

The stem लिङ्ग can be declined in *neuter* only. Here it is used in a compound and takes the *masculine* gender and must be spelled in 1st case singular.

Adjective विशेषण ।

स्त्रीलिङ्गः = पुंलिङ्गः , प्रथमा विभक्तिः , एकवचनम् । स्त्रीलिङ्गः m 1/1

The stem लिङ्ग can be declined in *neuter* only. Here it is used in a compound and takes the *masculine* gender and must be spelled in 1st case singular.

Numbers – Numerals

The numbers in Sanskrit i.e. सङ्ख्याः शब्दाः follow the English system of decimals, units, tens, hundreds, etc.

Just as we <u>count</u> 1, 2, 3 we count १, २, ३. This is known as cardinal numbering, as opposed to the method of counting first, second, third, which is known as ordinal numbering.

As is usual for nouns in Sanskrit, the numerals will follow gender and case and number.

Numerals	सङ्ख्याशब्दाः	stem	1st case
1	१	एक mfn	एकम्
2	२	द्वि mfn	द्वे dual
3	३	त्रि mfn	त्रीणि plural
4	४	चतुर् mfn	चत्वारि
5	५	पञ्चन्	पञ्च mfn
6	६	षष्	षट् mfn
7	७	सप्तन्	सप्त mfn
8	८	अष्टन्	अष्ट or अष्टौ
9	९	नवन्	नव mfn
10	१०	दशन्	दश mfn
11	११	एकादशन्	एकादश mfn
20	२०	विंशति f	विंशतिः
30	३०	त्रिंशत् f	त्रिंशत्
40	४०	चत्वारिंशत् f	चत्वारिंशत्
50	५०	पञ्चाशत् f	पञ्चाशत्
60	६०	षष्टि f	षष्टिः
70	७०	सप्तति f	सप्ततिः
80	८०	अशीति f	अशीतिः
90	९०	नवति f	नवतिः
100	१००	शत n	शतम्
1000	१०००	सहस्र n	सहस्रम्
10,000	१०,०००	अयुत n	अयुतम्

100,000	१ ० ० , ० ० ०	लक्ष n	लक्षम् lakh
10,00,000	१ ० , ० ० , ० ० ०	प्रयुत n	प्रयुतम् million
10000000	१ ० ० , ० ० , ० ० ०	कोटि f	कोटि: crore
10,0000000	१ ० ० ० , ० ० , ० ० ०	अर्बुद n	अर्बुदम्
100,0000000	१ ० , ० ० ० , ० ० , ० ० ०	अब्ज n	अब्जम् billion
1000,0000000	१ ० , ० ० ० , ० ० , ० ० ०	सहस्रकोटि=खर्व	खर्व:

Numbers – Cardinals

सङ्ख्या: शब्दा: = सङ्ख्याशब्दा:

Just as we may <u>write</u> cardinals in figures or in words, 1 or one, 2 or two, 3 or three, similarly in Sanskrit we write १ वा एकम्, २ वा द्वे, ३ वा त्रीणि ।

And now we highlight a difference, Sanskrit counting follows the gender of the item being counted, as

- एक: बाल: , one boy - *masculine*
- एका बाला , one girl - *feminine*
- एकम् फलम् , one fruit - *neuter*

An interesting fact here is that एकम् can have a sense other than "one". It can mean the article "a" in a sentence, as "a crowd". To account for such usage, the word एकम् can be declined in dual and plural as well. E.g. एके समूह: । It can also mean primary, sole, etc.

A sample Numeral Declension Chart

	one	two	five	twenty	thirty	hundred	crore
	neuter	n	mfn	feminine	f	n	f
	sing.	dual	plural	singular	sing.	sing.	sing.
1	एकम्	द्वे	पञ्च	विंशति:	त्रिंशत्	शतम्	कोटि:
2	एकम्	द्वे	पञ्च	विंशतिम्	त्रिंशतम्	शतम्	कोटिम्
3	एकेन	द्वाभ्यां	पञ्चभि:	विंशत्या	त्रिंशता	शतेन	कोट्या
4	एकस्मै	द्वाभ्यां	पञ्चभ्य:	विंशत्यै	त्रिंशते	शतस्मै	कोट्यै
5	एकस्मात्	द्वाभ्यां	पञ्चभ्य:	विंशत्या:	त्रिंशत:	शतस्मात्	कोट्या:
6	एकस्य	द्वयो:	पञ्चानाम्	विंशत्या:	त्रिंशत:	शतस्य	कोट्या:
7	एकस्मिन्	द्वयो:	पञ्चासु	विंशत्याम्	त्रिंशति	शतस्मिन्	कोट्यां

Numbers – Ordinals

Earlier we saw the numerals that are commonly referred to as the cardinals. Now we learn the ordinals, known as सङ्ख्येयशब्दाः or पूरणशब्दाः in Sanskrit. Cardinals are individual or isolated numbers as cash, whereas Ordinals refer to numbers in succession or in a series as in a sporting event.

Cardinals in figures	Cardinals in words	Ordinals in words	Ordinals in figures
1 – १	One एकम्	First प्रथमम्	1st
2 – २	Two द्वे	Second द्वितीयम्	2nd
100 – १००	Hundred शतम्	Hundredth शततमम्	100th
Ordinals decline in all genders, numbers, and cases			
Sample chart for three genders in nominative case singular			

	Mas पुंलिङ्गः	Fem स्त्रीलिङ्गः	Neu नपुंसकलिङ्गः
1st	प्रथमः	प्रथमा	प्रथमम्
2nd	द्वितीयः	द्वितीया	द्वितीयम्
100th	शततमः	शततमी	शततमम्

Numbers – How Many

कति सन्ति How many are there?

If we ask a question that has a numeric answer, the word used is कति – इकारान्तः शब्दः नित्यंबहुवचनान्तः त्रिषु लिङ्गेषु समानरूपः । It is इ-ending word, always in plural, same in all genders. However it is not an indeclinable since it shall decline in all the 7 cases.

How many apples? कति सेवफलानि ।
How many for the ladies? कतिभ्यः स्त्रीभ्यः ।
How many of the cars? कतिनाम् वाहनानाम् ।

Time and Date

We learnt the numerals, now we see how to tell the time. The word for clock is घटी and for o'clock वादनम् । For "am" we say प्रातः ।

8 o'clock am अष्ट–वादनम् प्रातः अष्टवादनम्

10 o'clock दश–वादनम् दशवादनम्

And a Quarter (15 minutes) स-पाद = सपाद, and a half (30 minutes) स–अर्ध = सार्ध , a Quarter to पाद–ऊन = पादोन ।

1:15pm सपाद–एक–वादनम् मध्याह्ने सपादएकवादनम्

3:30pm सार्ध–त्रि–वादनम् अपराहणे सार्धत्रिवादनम्

5:45am पादोन–षट्–वादनम् प्रातः पादोनषड्वादनम्

What is the time? कः समयः ।

When is the right time? कदा समीचीनः समयः ।

इदानीम् now	सप्ताहः week	पक्षः fortnight

अद्य today	मासः month	संवत्सरः year
श्वः tomorrow	परश्वः day after	आगामि in due course
ह्यः yesterday	परह्यः day before	गत the previous
वासरः day	सोमवासरः Monday	रविवासरः Sunday
Time is a very precise concept in Sanskrit literature, as it rules all beings and nature as well. The 24 hour day is traditionally split into 8 praharas प्रहरः of 3 hours each. A day is also divided into 30 muhurtas मुहूर्तः of 48 minutes each.		
प्रातः in morning, 4am to noon	मध्याह्ने in afternoon, Noon 12pm to 3pm, अपराह्णे 3pm – 6pm	रात्रौ at night-time, 9pm to 11:59pm midnight
उषा dawn	सायंकाले 6pm – 9pm	प्रदोषः dusk

Parts of Speech

There are eight parts of speech in language.

- Noun नाम = Person, Place, or Thing.
- Pronoun सर्वनाम = In place of a Noun already introduced.
- Verb क्रियापद = Action or State specifying word.
- Adverb क्रियाविशेषण = Describes the action more fully.
- Adjective विशेषण = Describes a noun or pronoun.
- Preposition विभक्ति = Establishes the purpose of the nouns.
- Conjunction समुच्चय = Connects words, clauses, sentences.
- Interjection उद्घोषण = Expression that lends emotion.

Parts of speech indicate how a word functions in meaning as well as in grammar within a sentence. The same word can function as a different part of speech when used in a different context. Understanding parts of speech is essential for determining the correct definition of a word when using a dictionary, and for understanding the correct import of a phrase or a sentence. Without knowing the parts of speech, we can easily mix the nouns and verbs, and wrongly interpret a text. And form a mistaken impression of someone or his statement.

<u>Analysis of Language</u>

- Lexical Analysis आनुपूर्वी = The process of breaking a sequence of characters into its **smallest meaningful unit**. E.g. words in a sentence, letters in a word, etc.
- Syntax शब्दानुशासनम् = is the process of identifying words according to rules of **grammar**, e.g. Verb, Noun.
- Morphology पदविश्लेषिका = the process of analyzing words into their **constituents**, viz. Root, Stem, Gender, Case, etc.
- Phonology शिक्षा वेदाङ्गम् = The science of sounds, as Phonetics is the classification of spoken sounds, how they are **uttered**.
- Semantics शब्दार्थः = Identifying **meaning** of a word or entity.

<u>Types of Sentences</u>

Declarative विधिविधानवाचकः , or Assertive, stating a fact.

Interrogative प्रश्नवाचकः , asking a question or seeking information.

Imperative आज्ञावाचकः , giving command or requesting permission.

Exclamatory विस्मयादिवाचकः, expressing emotion.

Vibhakti Kāraka Upapada विभक्तिः कारकः उपपदम्

We know Sanskrit is an inflectional language. The verbs and nouns are strongly inflected. The verbs undergo conjugation, and the nouns decline in various cases determined by context and usage in a sentence. These cases are known as Vibhakti. Vibhakti is of the following types:

- Karaka Vibhakti कारकः विभक्तिः i.e. कारकविभक्तिः
- Sambandha Vibhakti सम्बन्धः विभक्तिः i.e. सम्बन्धविभक्तिः
- Upapada Vibhakti उपपदं विभक्तिः i.e. उपपदविभक्तिः

<u>Karaka Vibhakti</u> कारकविभक्तिः is the case of the Noun in a sentence that is governed by the Verb, कारकः the impeller of action.
<u>Sambandha Vibhakti</u> सम्बन्धविभक्तिः is the case of the Noun in a sentence that is governed by सम्बन्धः the relationship with another Noun. <u>Upapada Vibhakti</u> उपपदविभक्तिः is the case of the Noun in a sentence that is governed by उपपदम् a supporting word.

Parts of a Sentence

A sentence may have many parts, some are outlined here.

Subject नामपदम् = Person, Place, or Thing., Object.

Predicate क्रियापदम् i.e. Verb that follows the Subject in gender, number, and case.

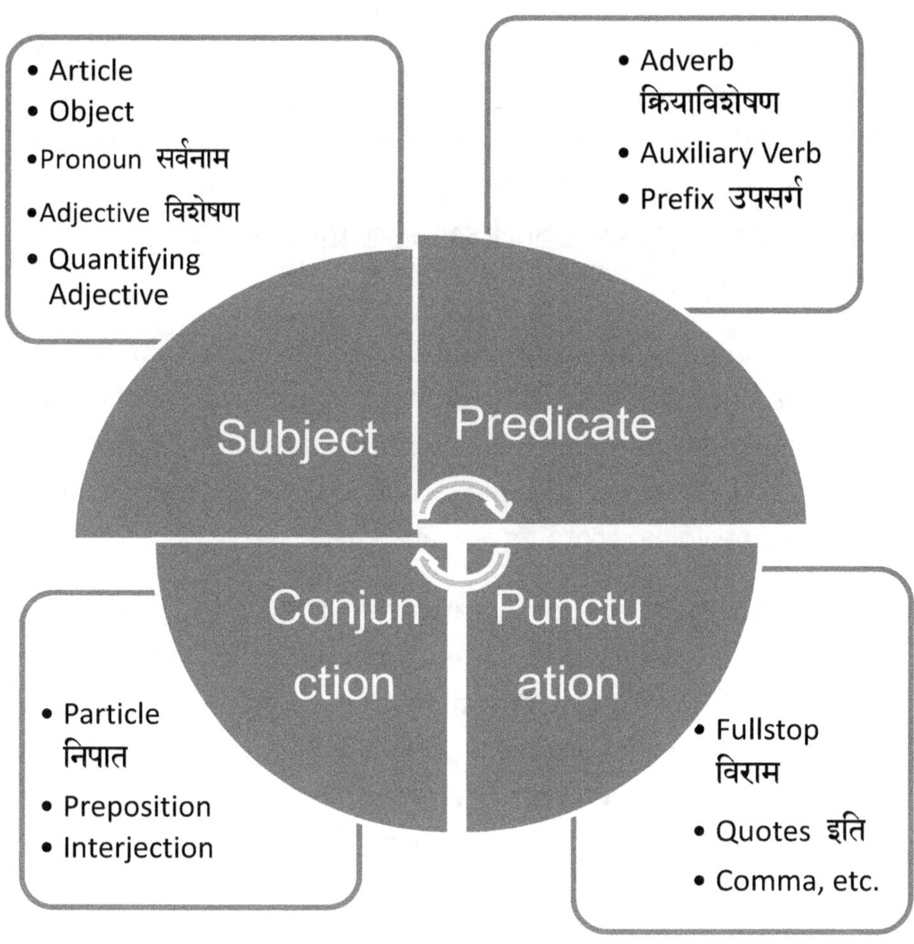

Sandhi - Blending of Adjacent Letters

Blending or mixing is common in life. Daily in cooking, to maintain relationships, and at work; we blend physical entities. Often our thoughts and imaginations are a blend of some sort.

Communication has a lion's share of blending of words. This is so well noticed when we hear <u>the same sentence</u> spoken by people of different cultures. On our own the mixing we do when speaking or communicating is rarely noticed by us, however, if we had to <u>write down exactly the way we said a sentence then the blend shall become very clear.</u>

It is not the tone or pitch or intonation or pronunciation that is being referred to. Rather it is the sentence that came out of the lips when written down exactly would seem to have a few spelling "mistakes" or "changes". Simply record your speech using your mobile phone voice recording app and check.

Some letters are "silent", others are uttered "differently" when speaking. Some letters seem to get combined, others are quite distinct, and few are affected by their preceding-or-succeeding letter! This is given the technical name SANDHI in Sanskrit grammar, i.e. the coalescence of adjacent letters or the modification in a letter due to the presence of a certain letter in the vicinity.

Sandhi is not about writing it differently and then speaking it. Rather, it is knowing fully well that a Spoken sentence could be different than its Written counterpart. Speech will naturally do some slight modification to certain words. *When these modifications are written down, then we call them Sandhi.*

In the case of English, this is no big deal, since we hardly ever change the written spelling of any word just because it sounds different in speech. In English, spellings follow the dictionary. Not so in the case of Sanskrit. Sanskrit evolved much before written scripts made their appearance. It was more or less an oral language for eons. Just as the speech of birds and bees is rarely written down. Just as the sounds of nature, the boom of the surf or the thunder is seldom put down in writing.

So when writing systems made their appearance, Sandhi was born. It was designed for new learners or non-native speakers to know exactly how to **speak the same word in different sentences**. Thus Sanskrit has this distinct advantage – one must utter what one sees in print.

e.g. Rama returns from the forest. रामः वनं आगच्छति ।

In Sanskrit we may write this sentence in various ways without ambiguity in meaning. However the pronunciation of the same word RAMA, undergoes changes, as in RAMAH, RAMO, RAMA.

रामः वनम् आगच्छति । Anusvara_prevented_before_a_vowel Sandhi.
रामो वनं आगच्छति । Visarga Sandhi.
राम आगच्छति वनम् । Visarga drop Sandhi.

Note – Lord Rama is conveniently and famously spelled in English literature as "Ram". In transliteration, the spelling is "Rāma". **This is due to evolution in writing scripts and fonts as the Unicode keeps getting updated, and Indian scripts are made available on the computer, smartphones, and in apps.**
Devanagari र्–आ–म्–अ = राम । Roman R-ā-m-a = Rāma.
The stem is राम Ram, whereas the protagonist is रामः Ramaḥ.

Sandhi – Change in Spelling/Pronunciation

A standalone word or a word in a dictionary has a spelling that can be at variance with the spelling of the same word seen in literature. Sandhi causes change in utterance and hence the change in spelling in print.

The grammar follows specific rules as to what should happen when letters of the alphabet meet each other at word boundaries in a sentence. This blending can be categorized as:
- Vowels meeting each other
- Consonants meeting each other
- The Visarga meeting a letter
- The Anusvara meeting a letter

Meeting of Vowels Sandhi

Simple Vowels अ , इ , उ , ऋ are lengthened to corresponding

Common Examples

सुर + इन्द्र	सुरेन्द्र	Surindar = a proper name
महा + ईश्वर	महेश्वर	Maheshwar = name of Lord
प्रति + एक:	प्रत्येक:	Each, everyone

Vowel अ followed by dissimilar vowel is strengthened to diphthong

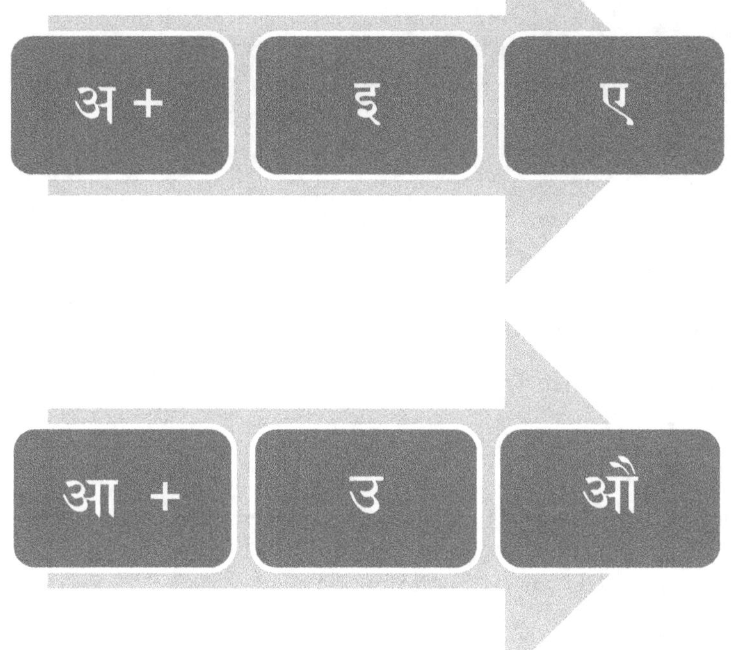

Vowel इ/उ followed by dissimilar vowel changes to semivowel य् / व्

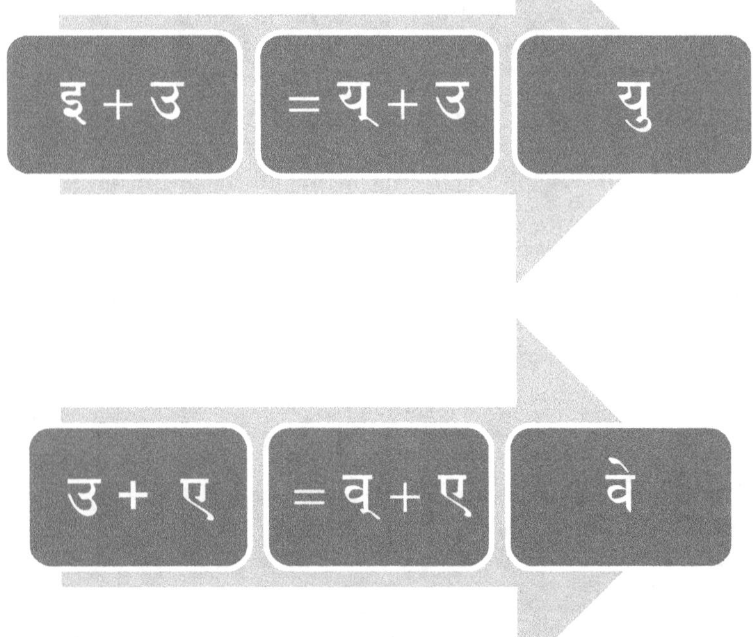

Similarly Diphthong ए/ऐ followed by any vowel changes to semivowel य् prefixed with अ/आ

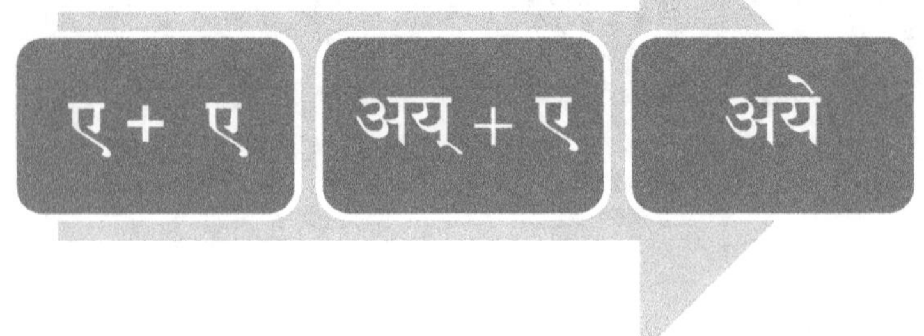

Similarly Diphthong ओ/औ followed by any vowel changes to semivowel व् prefixed with अ/आ

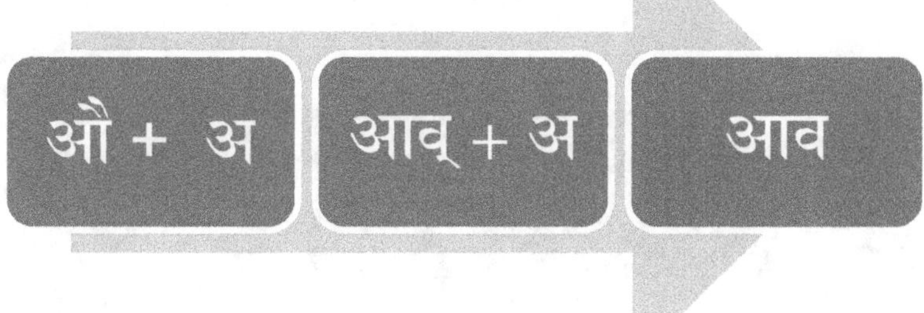

Adjacent Consonants Sandhi

Hard Dental letter त् is changed to Soft द् , e.g. भगवत् गीता = भगवद्गीता ।

Famous Colon Visarga Sandhi

Visarga is the sound of breath release, and it gets uttered as a vowel, e.g. as vowel ओ

Visarga uttered as sibilant श्

Mmm Anusvara Sandhi

Anusvara is uttered as a nasal म् , and results from म् or न् , e.g. सम् कृत = संस्कृत = Sanskrit. It is also uttered as a corresponding nasalized letter as seen.

The Sacred Sound = Om.

That which is well crafted. Made with Precision = Sanskrit.

Sentence Construction

A Sanskrit sentence follows the general syntax:

- SUBJECT OBJECT VERB.
- ADJECTIVE NOUN ADVERB VERB.

In other words, the verb is placed at the end in a sentence.
Boy to school goes.

The conjunctions च , नु , वा and the particles हि , उ , etc. are placed as the 2nd word in a sentence. **What and? This alone.**

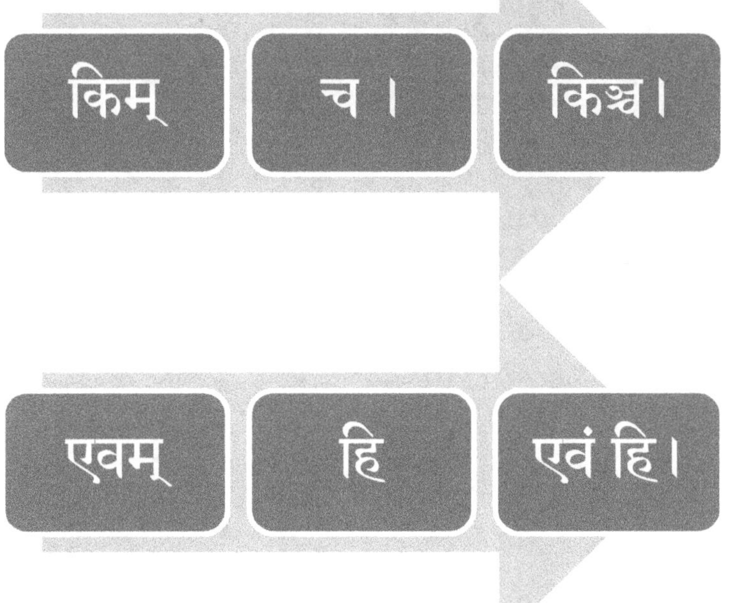

Spelling of Noun - Inflection

Nouns have the variable spelling in a sentence, as the preposition showing its place-holder is merged in the noun itself. If a noun is acting as a SUBJECT, it takes the Nominative case spelling. And if it is the OBJECT, its spelling changes to the Accusative case. Similarly change in spelling of the same noun to show it as the INSTRUMENT, or RECIPIENT, etc. Secondly, the noun will change its spelling based on gender and number. The same noun may be used to depict a masculine or a neuter gender, with appropriate change in its spelling.

Masculine word "Master" गुरुः Nominative case singular.
Neuter word "Heavy" गुरु Nominative case singular.

Many Masters are.

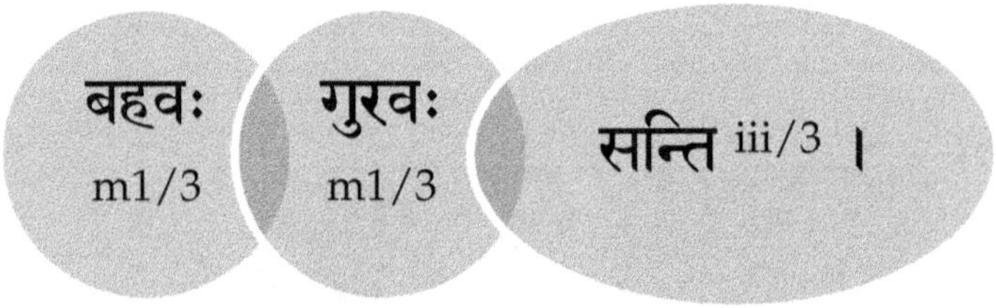

Goods Heavy are.

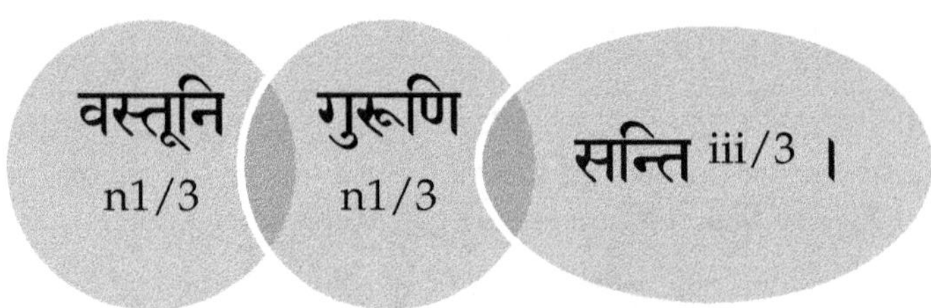

Spelling of Verb - Conjugation

Verbs maintain spelling across genders as in English. However their spelling changes with <u>number and person</u>, <u>tense and mood</u> as in English. The process of determining the correct spelling is known as Conjugation of Verbs.

Concordance of Subject and Verb

Spelling of noun as SUBJECT should match the number, i.e. singular-dual-plural, with the verb in a sentence. The noun in Nominative case should have the <u>same number</u> whether singular or plural as the verb in a sentence. For passive voice, Object matches the Verb, and Subject is in तृतीया विभक्तिः ।

Boy with a ball plays.

Boys with a ball play.

Boys with a ball played.

Concordance of Substantive and Adjective

Nouns in a sentence function as substantives and adjectives, since they represent words that can be perceived by the senses or understood by the intellect. Adjectives are nouns that qualify other nouns. The noun it qualifies is called a substantive. The Adjective in a sentence should have the same parameters of <u>gender</u>, <u>case</u>, and <u>number</u> as its Substantive. E.g. **Blue Sky is.**

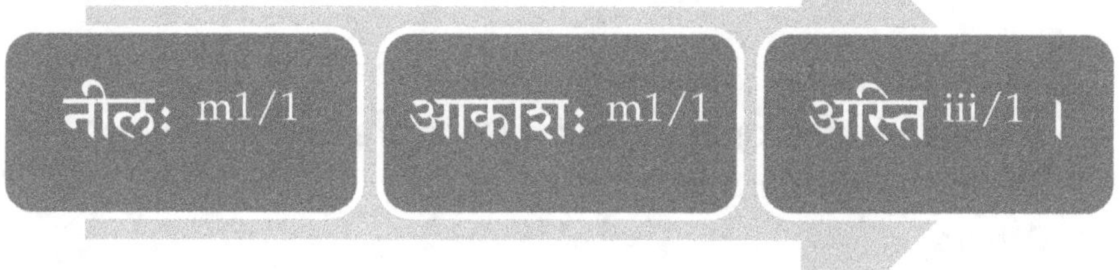

Blue Skies are.

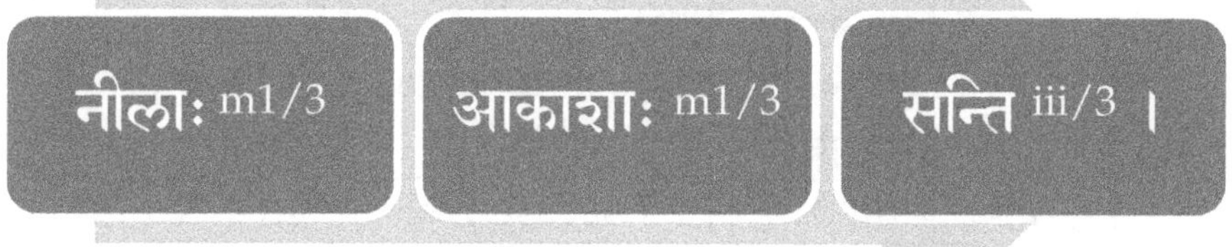

Blue Sky she sees.

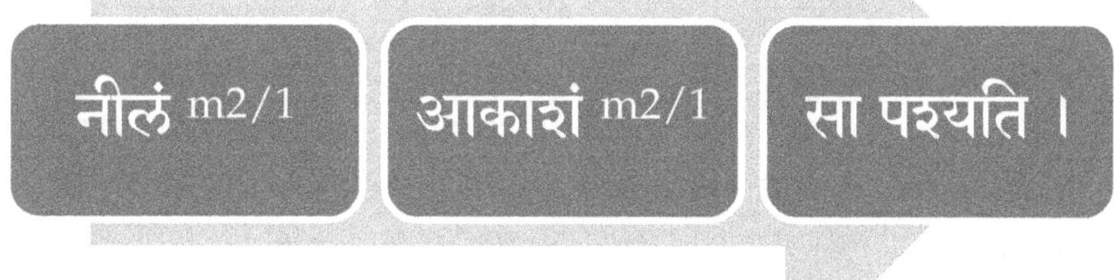

Upapada – Supporting or Subordinate Word

We have seen that Sanskrit is strongly inflected and that helps to place a word anywhere in a sentence without loss in meaning. There is the concept of words known as उपपदम् Upapada.

The उपपदम् word is used as a supporting word in a sentence. The Upapada <u>will decide the case</u> of the main word it supports. Hence the concept of Upapada Vibhakti, apart from Karaka Vibhakti.

The Upapada words fall into three categories
* Some are common prepositions and are indeclinables
* Some are standard Verbs
* Others

Sample Chart -Preposition Upapada words and cases they govern.

Upapada word	Main word	Case governed for Main word	Usage in a Sentence
सह with	रामः	3rd Instrumental	रामेण सह
विना without	अवलम्बनः	2nd Accusative	अवलम्बनं विना
	दुःखः	3rd Instrumental	दुःखेन विना
	उत्साहः	5th Ablative	उत्साहात् विना
उभतयः both sides	नगरः	2nd Accusative	नगरम् उभतयः
परितः all around	नगरः	2nd Accusative	नगरम् परितः
अलम् do not do	उत्तरम्	3rd Instrumental	उत्तरेण अलम्
अलम् enough of it	उत्तरम्	4th Dative	उत्तराय अलम्
नमः salute	शिवः	4th Dative	शिवाय नमः
बहिः outside	गृहम्	5th Ablative	गृहात् बहिः
पूर्वम् in front	गृहम्	5th Ablative	गृहात् पूर्वम्
परम् at back	गृहम्	5th Ablative	गृहात् परम्
उपरि on top of	आसनम्	6th Genitive	आसनस्य उपरि
अधः under	उत्पीठिका	6th Genitive	उत्पीठिकायाः अधः

सीता रामेण 3/1 सह upapada रमते । Sita delights with Rama.

उत्तरेण 3/1 अलम् upapada । Shh! Do not answer.

उत्तराय 4/1 अलम् upapada । Ah! Enough of answer.

Sample Chart of verbal Upapada words and the cases they govern.

Upapada word	Main word	Case governed for Main word	Usage in a Sentence
स्निह्यति in love	युवती	7th Locative	युवत्यां स्निह्यति
विश्वसिति faith in	शास्त्रम्	7th Locative	शास्त्रि विश्वसिति
क्रुध्यति angry at	माता	4th Dative	मात्रे क्रुध्यति
असूयति with jealousy	सुन्दरी	4th Dative	सुन्दरायै असूयति
रोचते enjoys	लड्डुकम्	4th Dative	लड्डुकाय रोचते

बालकः युवत्यां [7/1] स्निह्यति [upapada] । Boy loves girl.

बालकः लड्डुकाय [4/1] रोचते [upapada] । Boy enjoys sweetmeat.

Indeclinables

Words that do not change spelling at all are called Indeclinables. In Sanskrit, the nouns and verbs are all usually inflected. In a sentence, a word that isn't inflected is called an indeclinable. There are many such words in literature. Indeclinables are called Avyaya अव्ययम् । अव्ययानि ।

Infinitives

तुमुन् प्रत्यय–अन्तः शब्दः ।

Words used in the sense of the root form of a verb, viz. **to do** are called infinitives. These words express a wish or the intention to do something and are thus verbs. In Sanskrit these are made with the तुमुन् affix, and can be identified with their तुम् ending. Such words are indeclinables. **Girls to sing wish.**

Boys to play requested.

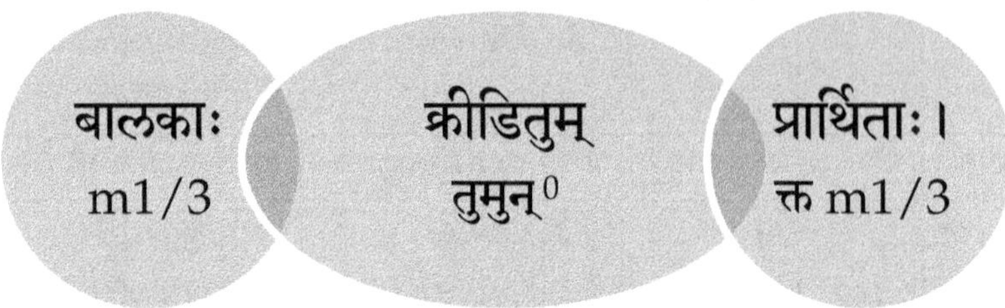

Adverbs

क्रिया विशेषण–शब्दः ।

Words that qualify verbs are called Adverbs. In Sanskrit the adverbs are generally indeclinable.

अकस्मात् suddenly	वर्षा अकस्मात् भवति ।
अचिरात् recently	हेमस्वरूपा अचिरात् आगच्छत् ।
उच्चैः loudly	संगीता–ऋचे उचैः भाषेते ।
शनैः softly	गुरवः शनैः वदन्ति ।
तूष्णीम् silently	हे शिशो ! तूष्णीम् पठ ।
तूष्णीम् silently	हे शिशू ! तूष्णीम् पठतम् ।
तूष्णीम् silently	हे शिशवः ! तूष्णीम् पठत ।

Particles

निपात

A particle is a tiny word that has a grammatical function but does not fit into the main parts of speech, i.e. it is not an adjective, noun, verb, or adverb. However it is a very important part of speech, and can alter the entire meaning of a sentence. It is used to lend weight, assertiveness, clarity, or emotion to a sentence.

अथ अपि इति इव एव क्वचित् खलु च तु वा ननु पुनः हि किम् ।

अथ word used to begin a speech or a sacred text	स्म added to a present tense verb to give the sense of past

किञ्च moreover. Placed at the head of a Sanskrit sentence.	tense. It is the last word in a Sanskrit sentence after the verb.
आम् yes, affirmative answer न no, negative answer	च and , वा or , तु but
मा do not	चेत् if , नोचेत् if not
खलु O Yes , हि verily , वै surely	ननु besides , अपि even
चित् , चन are joined to किम् to make "someone", "something", "whatever" किंचित् , केचित् , कश्चन , केचन sense of indefinite.	

Generally a particle is placed as the second word in a Sanskrit sentence. असतो मा सद्गमय । Lead me from Untruth to Truth.

A sample Literal translation = May I not fall into ignorance. May I traverse the path of wisdom.

Conjunctions

Conjunctions are short words that help in connecting two or more similar words or clauses in a sentence. These are indeclinables.

In English the conjunctions are placed between the words they connect, in Sanskrit they are placed between the words or at the end of those words. E.g.

Ram **and** Lakshman **and** Sita = राम **च** लक्ष्मण **च** सीता / राम लक्ष्मण सीता **च** । Day **or** Night = दिन **वा** रात्रि / दिन रात्रि **वा** ।
Beautiful **but** heartless = सुन्दरी **किन्तु** निर्दयी ।

Prepositions

Preposition is a word governing and expressing a relation to another word or entity in a sentence. In Sanskrit the prepositions are affixed to the nouns and are within a noun's spelling, so they do not govern the placement of nouns in the sentence. Still, we may use certain independent words as propositions to enhance the meaning of a sentence.

खलु O Yes, हि verily, वै surely, ननु besides, अपि even.

Interjections

Ejaculations, expressions of surprise or wonder, etc. are indeclinable. O, Wow वाह, Verily हि, Eh वै, Hey हे !

Svasti svāhā vaṣaṭ

स्वस्ति । स्वाहा । वषट् । Indeclinables chanted frequently during a Puja or Yagya ceremony. These signify स्वस्ति auspiciousness, स्वाहा offering, वषट् become mine.

Kāraka – Impeller of Action

Any <u>word</u> in a sentence that has a direct bearing on the <u>verb</u> is termed as कारकः karaka. Literally "karaka" means the one that impels action. Earlier we have seen the various cases विभक्तिः that govern the sense of nouns in a sentence. A noun in a sentence can behave as the Subject, Object, Instrument, etc. This behavior of the Noun is termed as कारकः in Sanskrit.

Since this behavior is closely associated with the *case* of the Noun, we say that कारकः governs the case of a Noun. Thus there is the concept of कारकः विभक्तिः = कारकविभक्तिः ।

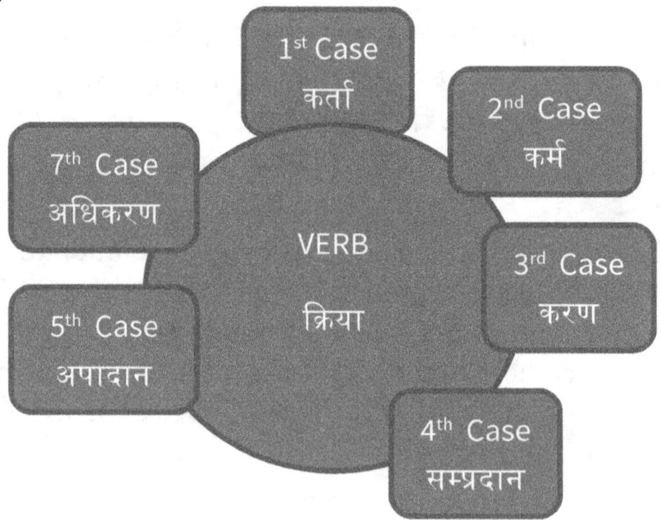

Rama goes to temple from home by car on Sunday for worship

रामः [m1/1] रविवासरे [m7/1] गृहात् [n5/1] प्रार्थनायै [f4/1] वाहनेन [n3/1] मन्दिरं [n2/1] गच्छति ।

Notice that the 6th case is not a Karaka Vibhakti, since it does not connect to the Verb, rather it connects to a noun in the sentence.

Samāsa - Compound Words

समासः

When two or more words that seem to have a relationship and hence can be condensed into a single word that captures the essence, that is known as Samasa समासः , or the formation of a compound word.

The technical process involves dropping the case endings of all the intermediate words and retaining a single case ending depending upon the meaning of the final word.

Thus a Samasa is made from finished words or inflected words. It involves Sandhi many a time where applicable, to further shorten the final word.

In English we have many such occurrences of words, but we do not bother to technically unravel the process. Most such English words are hyphenated. Hyphens' main purpose is to glue words together. They notify the reader that two or more entities in a sentence are linked. Although there are rules and customs governing hyphens, there are also situations when writers insert them for clarity.

e.g. servant of the king = King's servant. राज्ञः पुरुषः इति राजपुरुषः ।
e.g. mind pacifying agent = mind-pacifier. मननात् त्रायते इति मन्त्रः ।
e.g. Seeta and Geeta = Seeta-Geeta. सीता च गीता इति सीतागीते ।
e.g. not true = untrue. न सत् इति असत् ।

Sanskrit compound words are classified according to the technical process of word formation. Some are given here.

- तत् पुरुष–समासः That person or thing. The second or last word is denoted and is given weight and thus it determines the meaning of the Compound. राजपुरुषः । गुरुदक्षिणा ।
- बहुव्रीहि–समासः Two words or a sentence that signifies something totally different from the words themselves. नीलकण्ठः Lord Shiva. पीताम्बरः Krishna. लम्बोदरः Ganesha.
- द्वन्द्व–समासः All words are alike and connected by "and/or". सीतागीते । सत्असतौ । धर्माधर्म ।
- अव्ययीभाव–समासः The sense that pervades is of the indeclinable. Generally the first word is an indeclinable (an Upasarga) and it joins to any word to make the Compound. सौभाग्यवती । आजीवनम् । निस्सारः ।
- कर्मधारय–समासः Combination of Adjective and Noun. महादेवः । महर्षिः । आम्रवृक्षः । गुरुदेवः ।
- द्विगु–समासः Combination of count and Noun. पञ्चवटी । नवरात्री । त्रिलोकः । पञ्चपात्रम् । शताब्दी ।
- नञ् तत्पुरुष–समासः Making an antonym by prefixing "not". अधर्मः । अनादिः । अनन्तम् ।
- अलुक्–समासः A Compound type where the case ending of first word is retained. यधिष्ठिरः । आत्मनेपदम् । वाचस्पतिः ।
- नित्य–समासः A Compound type where the individual words may be unrelated to the Compound.
- अनित्य–समासः A Compound type where the individual words can be split and the correct meaning is still retained.

Vṛtti – Final Word Formation Methodology

पदविधिः

The technical procedure involved in formation of finished words is termed as Vritti वृत्तिः in Sanskrit. Simply put, the methodology of condensing an explanation into one word is called Vritti.

There are five such pathways. We see here that this concept of Vritti does not take into account the formation of Verbs from primary

Roots धातवः, it only details the formation of Verbs from सनाद्यन्तधातवः secondary Roots.

- कृत्–वृत्तिः = Root + Krit Affix → Stem + Sup Affix → NOUN
- तद्धित–वृत्तिः = Stem + Taddhita Affix → Stem + Sup → NOUN
- समास–वृत्तिः = word+word merge → Stem + Sup Affix → NOUN
- एकशेष–वृत्तिः = noun + similar noun → Retaining one NOUN
- सनाद्यन्त–धातु–वृत्तिः = Root+San Affix→New Root+Ting → VERB

Sati Saptamī - Locative Absolute

This is a distinct term seen in literature. It is used to club two actions together in TIME. It is an alternate and beautiful usage for the expressions यदा, तदा When/Then, "during the time".

Such an action expressed in **locative** case is termed **sati saptami**. It will involve the usage of a **participle**, whether past participle or present participle, in locative case.

The term सति has come from the 2nd Conjugation Root 1065 अस भुवि to be. Stem सत् with present active participle शतृ it is सन् in nominative singular and declines as सति in locative singular.

When spring comes, flowers bloom.
वसन्तकाले सम्प्राप्ते पुष्पाणि विकसन्ति । Locative case of Subject वसन्तकाले m7/1 , & Locative of Past Passive Participle क्त as सम्प्राप्ते m7/1.

Rain spoils the match play.
वर्षायां f7/1 क्रीडन्ति m7/1 स्पर्धा विकुरुते । stem क्रीडत् , क्रीडन् शतृ present active participle.

यः स सर्वेषु भूतेषु नश्यत्सु न विनश्यति ॥ Bhagavad Gita 8.20
सर्वेषु भूतेषु n7/3 , नश्यत्सु n7/3 शतृ of stem नश्यत् ।

ते तं भुक्त्वा स्वर्गलोकं विशालं क्षीणे पुण्ये मर्त्यलोकं विशन्ति । B. Gita 9.21
क्षीणे n7/1 पुण्ये n7/1 , विशन्ति n7/1 शतृ of stem विशत् ।

Sārvadhātuka, Ārdhadhātuka Concept

सार्वधातुक, आर्धधातुक is an important concept in Sanskrit Grammar.
It is applied to mean

- A conjugation group out of the 10 Conjugational Groups
- An Affix depending on its initial letter
- A tense or mood out of the 10 Tenses and Moods in grammar

<u>Conjugation Groups गण: Classified</u>

These have been divided into 10 chapters. Each chapter consists of
a group of Roots. These are called the 10 Conjugational Groups,
named as 1c, 2c, 3c, 4c, 5c, 6c, 7c, 8c, 9c, 10c. For each group, there
is a specific modifying letter, known as the Gana Vikarana, that
helps in word construction. Thus the Gana Vikarana and the
Conjugational Group has a one-to-one relationship. Each Root shall
join with its Gana Vikarana to make an Anga or intermediate Entity
in word construction.

- Root + Gana Vikarana = Anga, called Entity in grammar
- धातु + गणविकरण = अङ्गम् ।
- E.g. भू + शप् = भव ।

In word construction, the first thing seen is the ending letter of a
Root. That is of utmost importance as that will undergo changes.
The next thing seen is the ending letter of the Entity.

- In our example the ending letter of the Entity भव = भ् अ व् अ
  is the vowel अ ।

The 10 conjugational groups are further classified as Sarvadhatuka
or Ardhadhatuka, depending on the ENDING letter of the Entity
composed of Root + Gana Vikarana.

- Sarvadhatuka = सार्वधातुक = सार्व–धातुक = ending in
  completeness, the vowel अ ।
- Ardhadhatuka = आर्धधातुक = आर्ध–धातुक = incomplete, not
  ending in the vowel अ ।

Thus the 10 Conjugational Groups are classified as

- Four Sarvadhatuka Conjugational groups, viz. 1c, 4c, 6c, 10c
- Six Ardhadhatuka Conjugational groups, 2c, 3c, 5c, 7c,8c, 9c.

Ting Shit Affix तिङ् शित् प्रत्यय and Rest Classified

The affixes used in word construction are classified as

- Affixes in the तिङ् प्रत्यय set beginning with ति and ending in letter ङ्, and those having श् as Tag letter शित् प्रत्यय are Sarvadhatuka affixes. E.g. Present Tense लट् iii/1 affix ति । Present Participle affix शतृ ।
- Rest of the affixes, are all Ardhadhatuka affixes. E.g. Future Tense लृट् Vikarana स्य । Past Participle affix क्त ।

Tense and Mood Affixes Classified

The affixes used in making Verbs are the affixes used for each of the 10 tenses and moods. Based on the initial letter classification, the affixes for the tenses and moods are also classified as

- Affix with initial letter त् or श् , तिङ् प्रत्यय , शित् प्रत्यय is a Sarvadhatuka affix, so the four tenses and moods, viz. Present Tense लट् , Imperfect Past Tense लङ् , Imperative Mood लोट् , Potential Mood विधि लिङ् , are named as the Sarvadhatuka Tenses and Moods.

- Affix without initial letter त् or श् , अतिङ् प्रत्यय , अशित् प्रत्यय is an Ardhadhatuka affix, so the six tenses and moods, viz. Future Tense लृट् , General Future Tense लुट् , Aorist Past Tense लुङ् , Perfect Past Tense लिट् , Benedictive Mood आशीर् लिङ्, Conditional Mood लृङ् are named as the Ardhadhatuka Tenses and Moods.

Guṇa, Vṛddhi गुण वृद्धि Concept

गुण , वृद्धि, is an important concept in Sanskrit Grammar. It indicates the changes to be applied during word construction.

- Guna Letters are अ , ए , ओ ।
- Vriddhi Letters are आ , ऐ , औ ।

The Sarvadhatuka affixes are known to cause Guna Vriddhi modifications only when the affix is a पित् प्रत्ययः , i.e. having the प् Tag letter.

The Ardhadhatuka affixes are known to cause Guna Vriddhi modifications always.

Pit, Apit पित् अपित् Concept

The Sarvadhatuka affixes are known to cause Guna Vriddhi modifications only when the affix is a पित् प्रत्ययः , i.e. having the प् Tag letter. The Ardhadhatuka affixes do not have this sub-classification. All Ardhadhatuka affixes may cause Guna or Viddhi. None of the Ardhadhatuka affixes contain the प् Tag letter.

Ajādi, Halādi अजादि हलादि Concept

Roots or Affixes or Stems that have initial letter अच् a vowel, are termed अच्–आदि = अजादि। Roots or Affixes that have initial letter हल् a consonant, are termed हल्–आदि = हलादि ।

Ajanta, Halanta अजन्त हलन्त Concept

Roots or Affixes or Stems that have final letter अच् a vowel, are termed अच्–अन्त = अचन्त । Roots or Affixes that have final letter हल् a consonant, are termed हल्–अन्त = हलन्त ।

Gaṇa Vikaraṇa, Vikaraṇa गणविकरण , विकरण

Let us understand these two words clearly

- Gana Vikarana गणविकरण is an affix that is used to classify the Dhatupatha into the 10 conjugational groups. For E.g. शप् – 1c, श्यन् – 4c, उ – 8c etc.
- Vikarana is a modifier affix that is independent of the conjugational groups. E.g. Present Participle affix शतृ । Future Tense लृट् Vikarana स्य । Passive Voice affix यक् ।

Change of Letter षत्व , णत्व

It is observed that for some Roots, Affixes, Stems,

- the letter स् changes to ष् । Known as षत्वम् ।
- the letter न् changes to ण् । Known as णत्वम् ।

Reduplication द्वित्व , अभ्यास

During word formation, a portion of the Root gets duplicated due to an Affix. This is known as द्वित्वम् । Happens for

- Roots of 3c Conjugational Group facing Sarvadhatuka Ting Affixes
- Any Root facing सन् Desiderative Affix
- Any Root facing लिट् Distant Past Tense Affix

After द्वित्वम् , we will have two identical portions. The first portion of the reduplicated is called अभ्यास , and the अभ्यास undergoes further modifications.

Augments अट् , तुक् , पुक्

During word formation, in few instances it is observed that a new letter got inserted. This is known as augment.

- आट् Augment gets prefixed to अजादि Roots with initial vowel, during formation of Verbs of Imperfect Past Tense लङ् , Aorist Past Tense लुङ् , and Conditional Mood लृङ् ।
- अट् Augment gets prefixed to all हलादि Roots with initial consonant, during formation of Verbs of Imperfect Past Tense लङ् , Aorist Past Tense लुङ् , Conditional Mood लृङ् ।
- तुक् Augment gets inserted and when it faces letter छ , it becomes च् , so we see the च्छ conjunct in some cases.
- पुक् Augment gets inserted.

Elements in Word Construction

Dhātu धातुः = Root , Anga अङ्गम् = Entity that faces an Affix

Prātipadika प्रातिपदिकम् = Stem , Pratyaya प्रत्ययः = Affix

Anubandha अनुबन्धः = TAG Letter (इत्)

Gana Vikaraṇa गण–विकरणः = Affix to Conjugational Groups

Vikaraṇa विकरणः = A modifier Affix

Sthani स्थानि = Portion that will undergo change

Ādesha आदेशः = A change ordained in a specific letter

Āgama आगमः = An addition ordained for a specific letter

Affixes

प्रत्ययः Pratyaya
An Affix is a grammatical entity in word construction. It is a letter or a combination of letters. Depending on where it is placed, it is called
- Suffix is an affix placed at the end
- Prefix is an affix placed at the beginning
- Infix is an affix placed somewhere in the middle

In Sanskrit, there is a single word for affix, प्रत्ययः Pratyaya.

Consider the Equation
A + B + C + D = Final Word (e.g. a Verb)
Since the starting point for every Sanskrit word is the Root, so we can say
- A + Root + C + D = Verb
- Prefix + Root + Suffix + Suffix = Verb
- Prefix + Root + Infix + Suffix = Verb

Suffixes to Roots to make Verbs – तिङ् 3x3 matrix

Suffixes to Roots to make Stems – कृत्

Suffixes to Stems to make Nouns – सुप् 7x3 matrix

Suffixes to Stems to make Stems – तद्धितः

Ting/Sup Affixes तिङन्त / सुबन्त – Final Word

All words in Sanskrit are made from Ting Affixes and Sup Affixes.

- The तिङन्त Ting Affixed words are Verbs. These can be conjugated in the 3x3 matrix.
- The सुबन्त Sup affixed words are Nouns. These will be declined in the 7x3 matrix.

K ṛt Affixes कृदन्त – Intermediate Stem

All प्रातिपदिक stems in Sanskrit are made from Krit Affixes, or Taddhita Affixes or Samasa-endings.

- The कृत् Krit Affixes get added to Roots. These कृदन्त Krit Affixed words are प्रातिपदिक Stems. These when suffixed with Sup affixes make Nouns.

Taddhita Affixes तद्धितन्त – Intermediate Stem

Taddhita तद्धित Affixes get added to Stems to make new Stems, तद्धितन्त । This process can be repeated to make newer stems.

- Root + कृत् Affix → कृदन्त + तद्धित Affix → तद्धितन्त + सुप् Affix → सुबन्त = Noun.
- Root + कृत् Affix → कृदन्त + तद्धित Affix → तद्धितन्त + तद्धितन्त → तद्धितन्त + सुप् Affix → सुबन्त = Noun.

Sanādi Affixes –New Root

- Root + Sanadi Affix → New Root + Ting Affix → Verb. . E.g. Stem + सन् प्रत्यय → New Root + Ting Affix → Verb.
- Stem + Sanadi Affix → New Root + Ting Affix → Verb. E.g. Stem + क्विप् प्रत्यय → New Root + Ting Affix → Verb.

The new root is called a secondary or derived root निष्पन्न धातुः ।

Denominative Root नाम धातु

There are some Sanadi affixes (e.g. क्विप्) out of the 12 affixes, which can be suffixed to Stems. In such cases the new Root is known as नाम धातु Denominative Root.

Sanādi Noun Construction

- Root + Sanadi Affix → New Root + Krit Affix → Stem + Sup Affix → Noun. E.g. Stem + सन् प्रत्यय → New Root + क्त प्रत्यय → Stem + Sup Affix → Noun.

Feminine Suffixes ङीष् टाप् -Intermediate Stem

All stems प्रातिपदिकम् are technically masculine. A specific feminine affix when added to it makes it a feminine stem, and then it can decline to make nouns according to the grammar rules in a 7x3 matrix. E.g. कुमार + ङीष् → कुमार + ई → कुमारी ^{feminine stem} I will decline as the template feminine stem नदी on addition of the सुप् affixes.

A text called the लिङ्गानुशासनम् Linganushasana details the gender of stems.

Neuter – no explicit Suffixes

For the formation of Neuter gender प्रातिपदिक stems and words, there aren't any suffixes different from the masculine. However some words and compounds are defined as Neuter gender in the Ashtadhyayi. And the rules for declining the neuter stems are given. Also the text लिङ्गानुशासनम् Linganushasana specifies stems according to gender.

Unādi Suffixes उण् -Intermediate Stem

These are a special class of affixes that are applied to Roots to make प्रातिपदिक Stems and are listed in the Ganapatha. Commentaries are available on the Unadi affixes. Some well-known words are made using these. E.g. लक्ष्मी Lakshmi, वाक् Speech, etc.

Upasarga - Root Prefix

As we know, Sanskrit has 1943 Roots, that are the basic building blocks of the language. The Ashtadhyayi of Panini in one of its sutras points to sounds known as the उपसर्गः Upasarga. These are Indeclinables and are seen in literature <u>prefixed to some Roots</u>

- that change the meaning of the Root significantly

- that add depth and intensity to the original meaning
- that make an antonym of the original Root
- that do not cause any change, i.e. serve as a synonym

These 22 sounds प्र परा अप सम् अनु अव निस् निर् दुस् दुर् वि आङ् नि अधि अपि अति सु उत् प्रति परि उप are listed in the "Ganapatha of Panini".

- Upasargas are prefixed to Roots, hence commonly observed in Verbs, however a few Nouns also have Upasargas.
- Two or more Upasargas may be joined and prefixed.
- Upasargas change the क्त्वा affix to ल्यप् affix for a Root.
- Some Upasargas change the attribute from Atmanepadi to Parasmaipadi or vice versa for certain Roots.
- By Sandhi Rules दुर् , दुस् and निर् , निस् may be taken as the same, so some books list 20 Upasargas.
- Due to Sandhi उत् is seen as उद् also.
- In usage आङ् is seen as आ, since ङ् is a tag letter.

अति extreme	अव below	नि into	प्रति oppose
अधि above	आङ् upto	निर् without	वि special
अनु follow	उत् upon	निस् from	सम् with
अप away	उप subordinate	परा opposite	सु good
अपि also	दुर् hard	परि around	
अभि towards	दुस् bad	प्र much	

Examples

अनुकूलः convenient	गच्छ् to go गच्छति goes आगच्छति comes
प्रतिकूलः inconvenient	उप–नि–षद् उपनिषद् Upanishad

Some more sounds are seen prefixed to Roots, namely, अलम् बहिस् अन्तर् स्वी उष्णी सज्जी आविर् तिरस् अस्तम् ऊरी

Roots in Sanskrit

Primary Roots from the Dhatupatha

Primary Roots सौत्र धातवः from the Ashtadhyayi

Secondary Roots सनादि धातवः from the Ashtadhyayi

Root Attributes

Parasmaipada-Atmanepada-Ubhayepada Attribute

- Parasmaipada = General Action or for someone else
- Atmanepada = Action for Oneself
- Ubhayepada = Action in either Sense

Sakarmaka-Akarmaka-Dvikarmaka Attribute

- सकर्मक = Transitive, Verb that takes an Object
- अकर्मक = Intransitive, Verb that doesn't take any Object
- द्विकर्मक = Verb that takes two Objects.

Set-Anit-Vet Attribute सेट् अनिट् वेट्

These are the attributes that show up in Verbs and Nouns. Only some affixes use this attribute. E.g. Present Tense लट् doesn't use this attribute whereas Simple Future Tense लृट् uses it.

The 10 Conjugational Groups

The Dhatupatha contains ten conjugational groups, the gana vikarana गण-विकरण is common for each group, for the sarvadhatuka सार्वधातुक conjugational tenses & moods; Lat, Lot, Lang & VidhiLing.

SN	Dhatu	Meaning	Gana Vikarana	Without Tag	Conjugation Group name & No	
1	भू	सत्तायाम्	शप्	अ	भवादि-गण	1c
1011	अद	भक्षणे	शप् – लुक्	-	अदादि-गण	2c
1083	हु	दान-अदानयोः	शप् – श्लु	-	जुहोत्यादि-गण	3c
1107	दिवु	क्रीडा॰	श्यन्	य	दिवादि-गण	4c
1247	षुञ्	अभिषवे	श्नु	नु	स्वादि-गण	5c
1281	तुद	व्यथने	श	अ	तुदादि-गण	6c
1438	रुधिर्	आवरणे	श्नम्	न	रुधादि-गण	7c
1463	तनु	विस्तारे	उ	उ	तनादि-गण	8c
1473	डुक्रीञ्	द्रव्य-विनिमये	श्ना	ना	क्र्यादि-गण	9c
1534	चुर	स्तेये	णिच् + शप्	अय	चुरादि-गण	10c

Note - For the six Ardhadhatuka आर्धधातुक tenses and moods; Lit, Lut, LRt, AshirLing, Lung & LRng, all the 1943 Roots are one set and not ten groups as above.

Anatomy of Verb

The 3x3 Matrix for person and number

Third person = He, She, It (in any gender, Verb remains the same)
Second = You (irrespective of gender)
First Person = I (irrespective of gender)

Singular number = Subject is single.
Dual number = Subject is two things or peoples.
Plural number = Subject is three or more in number.

No Gender Attribute

Active Voice, Passive and Impersonal Voice

The 10 Tenses and Moods

Verb Construction Flow Chart

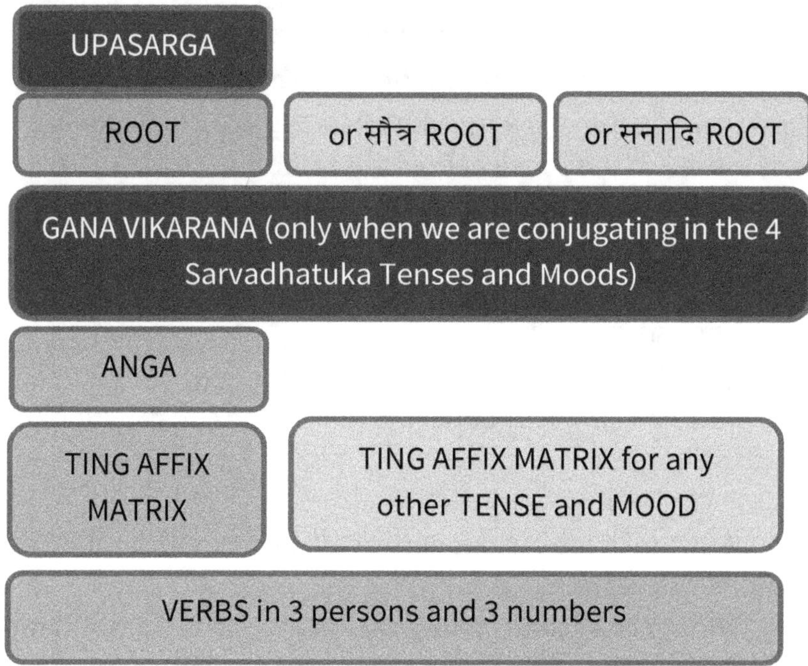

Verb Tenses and Moods

1	लट्	Present Tense
2	लुङ्	Aorist Past Tense – *before from now onwards*
3	लङ्	Imperfect Past Tense – *before from yesterday onwards*
4	लिट्	Perfect Past Tense – *distant unseen past* (also known as Distant Past Tense)
5	लृट्	Simple Future Tense – *now onwards*
6	लुट्	Periphrastic Future Tense – *tomorrow onwards*
7	लृङ्	Conditional Mood – *if/then in past or future sense*
8	लोट्	Imperative Mood – *request*
9	विधि–लिङ्	Potential Mood – *order* विधिलिङ् (also known as Optative Mood)
10	आशीर्–लिङ्	Benedictive Mood – *blessing* आशीर्लिङ् (also used in the sense of a curse)

There is an additional lakara, known as लेट् seen in Vedic use. It is used in the sense of Potential Mood.

Earlier we saw the concepts of

- सार्वधातुक , आर्धधातुक
- गुण , वृद्धि
- पित् , अपित्
- गणविकरण , विकरण

A firm grounding in these concepts makes the construction of Verbs smooth sailing.

लकार: ꠟ Sanskrit uses various sets of affixes to indicate the Tense and Mood in question.

- The set of affixes is known as लकार: , since a grammatical term "ल" has been defined to call such affixes.

- These affixes are known as तिङ् Ting affixes, since the first affix in this set starts with ति , and the last affix ends in the ङ् letter.
- The set of affixes for the Present Tense is named लट् लकारः ।

The primary affixes are 9 in number for a Root, that help to make Verbs indicating a general action, Parasmaipadi. A separate set of 9 affixes are used to make Verbs that indicate specifically that the action being done is for oneself, Atmanepadi. Thus there are 18 affixes in all in the set, the first one is तिप् , the last one is महिङ् ।

Note – The sense of Parasmaipada and Atmanepada was followed in the Vedic literature as evident in the Upanishads. However it got diluted in the classical literature as evident in the Ramayana, and it is not really applied in the modern context when framing a sentence. Only the correct affix, whether Parasmaipada or Atmanepada, continues to be used; the sense is immaterial.

E.g.
I walk to school. अहं विद्यालयं गच्छति । अहं विद्यालयं चरति ।

The Root for "to walk" was correctly selected from the Dhatupatha. If the sense was "I walk for my sake", then the Root selected was गम् । However if the sense was "I walk since I have been summoned or called" then the Root chosen was चर् । Also, the Root चर् was used when the sense was not important, i.e. general use.

There are 9 affixes since each Verb will be conjugated in a 3x3 matrix. Here 3 refers to person – third person, second person, first person. And 3 refers to number – singular, dual, plural.

Notice that Verbs do not have a gender attribute. It means the same Verb will be used irrespective of the gender of the subject or object. E.g. सः गच्छति । He goes. सा गच्छति She goes । तत् गच्छति । It goes.

The set of 9 Ting Affixes that make a Verb get modified based on

- The Root, whether it is Parasmaipadi or Atmanepadi.
- Conjugational Group of Root, Regular or Irregular gana.
- Tense or Mood to be applied, Present tense, Past Tense, etc.
- Active Voice or Passive Voice to be applied.
- Specific sutra from the Ashtadhyayi in few cases.
- Sandhi rules.

Present Tense

लट्

Having made the primary Ting affixes Chart for all tenses and moods, and all conjugational groups, Panini then introduced slight modifications as he observed the actual Verbs used in Literature.

Affixes Matrix primary

Ting Affixes Chart with place holders based on person and number.

तिङ् प्रत्यय:	General Action "Parasmaipadi"			Action for oneself "Atmanepadi"		
Person	Singular	Dual	Plural	Singular	Dual	Plural
3rd	तिप् iii/1	तस् iii/2	झिiii/3	त iii/1	आताम्iii/2	झ iii/3
2nd	सिप् ii/1	थस् ii/2	थ ii/3	थास् ii/2	आथाम् ii/2	ध्वम् ii/3
1st	मिप् i/1	वस् i/2	मस्i/3	इट् i/1	वहि i/2	महिङ्i/3

Present Tense Active Voice Chart in actual use.
Regular Ganas 1c,4c,6c,10c. लट् कर्त्तरि प्रयोगः

तिङ् प्रत्यय:	General Action "Parasmaipadi"			Action for oneself "Atmanepadi"		
Person	Singular	Dual	Plural	Singular	Dual	Plural
3rd	तिप् iii/1	तस् iii/2	अन्ति	ते iii/1	इते iii/2	अन्ते
2nd	सिप् ii/1	थस् ii/2	थ ii/3	से ii/2	इथे ii/2	ध्वे ii/3
1st	मिप् i/1	वस् i/2	मस् i/3	ए i/1	वहे i/2	महे i/3

Present Tense Chart - irRegular Ganas 2c, 3c, 5c, 7c, 8c, 9c. लट् कर्त्तरि

तिङ् प्रत्यय:	General Action "Parasmaipadi"			Action for oneself "Atmanepadi"		
Person	Singular	Dual	Plural	Singular	Dual	Plural
3rd	तिप् iii/1	तस् iii/2	अन्ति	ते iii/1	आते iii/2	अते *
2nd	सिप् ii/1	थस् ii/2	थ ii/3	से ii/2	आथे ii/2	ध्वे ii/3
1st	मिप् i/1	वस् i/2	मस् i/3	ए i/1	वहे i/2	महे i/3

*Note – There is one change here. For the 3rd conjugational group 3c, the 3rd person plural Ting Affix for Atmanepadi will be अति ।

The above charts have the special letter known as Tag letter in Panini Grammar. These Tag letters serve as catalysts to change the grammatical equations when needed, and then get dropped. The Tag letters are hence termed "invisible", their force is seen, but they themselves are not seen.

Affixes Matrix primary without Tag

Present Tense Active Voice Chart without Tag letters - Regular Ganas 1c, 4c, 6c, 10c. लट् कर्त्तरि प्रयोग:

तिङ् प्रत्यय:	General Action "Parasmaipadi"			Action for oneself "Atmanepadi"		
Person	Singular	Dual	Plural	Singular	Dual	Plural
3rd	ति	तस्	अन्ति	ते	इते	अन्ते
2nd	सि	थस्	थ	से	इथे	ध्वे
1st	मि	वस्	मस्	ए	वहे	महे

Present Tense Active Voice Chart without Tag letters - irRegular Ganas 2c, 3c, 5c, 7c, 8c, 9c. लट् कर्त्तरि प्रयोग:

तिङ् प्रत्यय:	General Action "Parasmaipadi" * अति for 3c.			Action for oneself "Atmanepadi"		
Person	Singular	Dual	Plural	Singular	Dual	Plural
3rd	ति	तस्	अन्ति*	ते	आते	अते
2nd	सि	थस्	थ	से	आथे	ध्वे
1st	मि	वस्	मस्	ए	वहे	महे

Due to Sandhi, there are further changes. We show the charts taking into account modifications by Sandhi.

Chart without Tags - Regular Ganas 1c, 4c, 6c, 10c. Sandhi Modifications.

लट् कर्त्तरि प्रयोग: Present Tense Active Voice

तिङ् प्रत्यय:	General Action "Parasmaipadi"			Action for oneself "Atmanepadi"		
Person	Singular	Dual	Plural	Singular	Dual	Plural
3rd	ति	त:	अन्ति	ते	इते	अन्ते
2nd	सि	थ:	थ	से	इथे	ध्वे
1st	आमि	आव:	आम:	ए	वहे	महे

Present Tense Active Voice Chart without Tag letters - irRegular Ganas 2c, 3c, 5c, 7c, 8c, 9c. लट् कर्त्तरि प्रयोग:

तिङ् प्रत्यय:	General Action "Parasmaipadi" * अति for 3c.			Action for oneself "Atmanepadi"		
Person	Singular	Dual	Plural	Singular	Dual	Plural
3rd	ति	तस्	अन्ति*	ते	आते	अते
2nd	सि	थस्	थ	से	आथे	ध्वे
1st	मि	वस्	मस्	ए	वहे	महे

Verb Conjugation Matrix भू

Present Tense Active Voice Verbs लट् कर्त्तरि प्रयोग: क्रियापदानि

Root+Affix	भू 1cP , भव Anga ready for Conjugation		
Person	Singular	Dual	Plural
3rd	भव + ति	भव + त:	भव + अन्ति
2nd	भव + सि	भव + थ:	भव + थ
1st	भव + आमि	भव + आव:	भव + आम:

Sentences using Verbs made from भू सत्तायाम् 1cP = to exist

Sentences	भू 1cP , भव Anga ready for Conjugation		
Person	Singular	Dual	Plural

3rd	सः भवति । He is.	तौ भवतः । They both are.	ते भवन्ति । They are.
2nd	त्वं भवसि । You are.	युवाम् भवथः । You two are.	यूयम् भवथ । You are.
1st	अहं भवामि । I am.	आवां भवावः । We both are.	वयं भवामः । We are.

Verb Conjugation Matrix लभ् 1cA -to get

Present Tense Active Voice Verbs लट् कर्त्तरि प्रयोगः क्रियापदानि

Verbs	लभ् प्राप्तौ 1cA = to get		
Person	Singular	Dual	Plural
3rd	लभते	लभेते	लभन्ते
2nd	लभसे	लभेथे	लभध्वे
1st	लभे	लभावहे	लभामहे

Verb Conjugation Matrix दा 3cU –to give

Present Tense Active Voice Verbs लट् कर्त्तरि प्रयोगः क्रियापदानि

Root+Affix	दा 3cU –Irregular Gana-Parasmaipada Chart		
Person	Singular	Dual	Plural
3rd	दा + ति	दा + तः	दा + अति
2nd	दा + सि	दा + थः	दा + थ
1st	दा + आमि	दा + वः	दा + मः

Verbs	दा 3cU –Irregular Gana-Parasmaipada Chart		
Person	Singular	Dual	Plural
3rd	ददाति	दत्तः	ददति
2nd	ददासि	दत्थः	दत्थ
1st	ददामि	दद्वः	दद्मः

Sentences using Verbs made from दा दाने 3cU = to give

Sentences	दा 3cU –Irregular Gana-Parasmaipada Chart		
Person	Singular	Dual	Plural

3rd	सः ददाति । He gives.	तौ दत्तः । They both give.	ते ददति । They give.
2nd	त्वं ददासि । You give.	युवाम् दत्थः । You two give.	यूयम् दत्थ । You give.
1st	अहं ददामि । I give.	आवां दद्वः । We both give.	वयं दद्मः । We give.

Root+Affix	दा 3cU – Irregular Gana - Atmanepada Chart		
Person	Singular	Dual	Plural
3rd	दा + ते	दा + आते	दा + अते
2nd	दा + से	दा + आथे	दा + ध्वे
1st	दा + ए	दा + वहे	दा + महे

Verbs	दा 3cU – Irregular Gana - Atmanepada Chart		
Person	Singular	Dual	Plural
3rd	दत्ते	ददाते	ददते
2nd	दत्से	ददाथे	दध्वे
1st	ददे	दद्वहे	दद्महे

Sentences using Verbs made from दा दाने 3cU = to give

Sentences	दा 3cU – Irregular Gana - Atmanepada Chart		
Person	Singular	Dual	Plural
3rd	सः दत्ते । He gives.	तौ ददाते । They both give.	ते ददते । They give.
2nd	त्वं दत्से । You give.	युवाम् ददाथे । You two give.	यूयम् दध्वे । You give.
1st	अहं ददे । I give.	आवां दद्वहे । We both give.	वयं दद्मे । We give.

We see here that even though the Verbs are conjugated in both Parasmaipada and Atmanepada, and hence have different spellings, their meaning remains the same. Perhaps in the Vedic era the meaning was differentiated with the sense of "mineness" and hence

सः ददाति probably meant "he gives" "*for someone else's use or general use*",
while
सः दत्ते probably meant "he gives" "*for his own use*".

Verb Conjugation Matrix शम् 4cP –to be calm

Present Tense Active Voice Verbs लट् कर्त्तरि प्रयोगः क्रियापदानि

Verbs	शम् 4cP , शाम्य Anga ready for Conjugation		
Person	Singular	Dual	Plural
3rd	शाम्यति	शाम्यतः	शाम्यन्ति
2nd	शाम्यसि	शाम्यथः	शाम्यथ
1st	शाम्यामि	शाम्यावः	शाम्यामः

Verb Conjugation Matrix कृ 8cU –to do, to make

Present Tense Active Voice Verbs लट् कर्त्तरि प्रयोगः क्रियापदानि

Verbs	कृ 8cU -Irregular Gana -Parasmaipada Chart		
Person	Singular	Dual	Plural
3rd	करोति	कुरुतः	कुर्वन्ति
2nd	करोषि	कुरुथः	कुरुथ
1st	करोमि	कुर्वः	कुर्मः

Verbs	कृ 8cU - Irregular Gana - Atmanepada Chart		
Person	Singular	Dual	Plural
3rd	कुरुते	कुर्वाते	कुर्वते
2nd	कुरुषे	कुर्वाथे	कुरुध्वे
1st	कुर्वे	कुर्वहे	कुर्महे

We have seen the sentences सः करोति and सः कुरुते made using the Parasmaipada and Atmanepada affixes respectively. The spelling varies, however the meaning is identical in the modern usage.

Past Tense

Sanskrit has three types of Past Tense usages, since it came into existence in the early dawn of time, and the early grammarians conceived of

- लिट् Past Tense event that no one had seen.
- लङ् Past Tense event that could simply be said belonging to yesterday or before that, and which was certainly witnessed by someone.
- लुङ् Past Tense that was in the fraction of the moment just gone by. This was also extended to mean the time span before that moment also. This event was certainly seen by the narrator or speech giver himself, (besides others).

Imperfect Past Tense

लङ् = Past tense other than today, i.e. yesterday and before. This is the most common past tense used in the modern context. It has a notable feature that each Verb begins with the vowel अ , due to the prefixing of the अट् augment. In Roots which are themselves vowel beginning, the Verbs are prefixed with आट् ।

Verb Conjugation Matrix भू

Imperfect Past Tense Active Voice Verbs लङ् कर्त्तरि प्रयोगः क्रियापदानि

Root+Affix	भू 1cP , भव Anga ready for Conjugation		
Person	Singular	Dual	Plural
3rd	अ + भव + त्	अ + भव + ताम्	अ + भव् + अन्
2nd	अ + भव + स्	अ + भव + तम्	अ + भव + त
1st	अ + भव् + अम्	अ + भवा + व	अ + भवा + म

The iii/3, i/1 forms; and i/2, i/3 forms; have Sandhis applied.

Verbs	भू सत्तायाम् 1cP = to be, to exist		
Person	Singular	Dual	Plural
3rd	अभवत्	अभवताम्	अभवन्
2nd	अभवः	अभवतम्	अभवत
1st	अभवम्	अभवाव	अभवाम

Verb Conjugation Matrix लभ्

Imperfect Past Tense Active Voice Verbs लङ् कर्त्तरि प्रयोगः क्रियापदानि

Root+Affix	लभ् 1cA , लभ Anga ready for Conjugation		
Person	Singular	Dual	Plural
3rd	अ + लभ + त	अ + लभ + इताम्	अ + लभ् + अन्त
2nd	अ + लभ + थाः	अ + लभ + इथाम्	अ + लभ + ध्वम्
1st	अ + लभ + इ	अ + लभा + वहि	अ + लभा + महि

The iii/3 form; and i/2, i/3 forms; have Sandhis applied to Anga.

Verbs	लभ् 1cA , लभ Anga ready for Conjugation		
Person	Singular	Dual	Plural
3rd	अलभत	अलभेताम्	अलभन्त
2nd	अलभथाः	अलभेथाम्	अलभध्वम्
1st	अलभे	अलभावहि	अलभामहि

Verb Conjugation Matrix दा

Imperfect Past Tense Active Voice Verbs लङ् कर्त्तरि प्रयोगः क्रियापदानि

Root+Affix	दा 3cU –Irregular Gana-Parasmaipada Chart		
Person	Singular	Dual	Plural
3rd	अ+ दा + त्	अ+ दा + ताम्	अ+ दा + उः
2nd	अ+ दा + स्	अ+ दा + तम्	अ+ दा + त
1st	अ+ दा + अम्	अ+ दा + व	अ+ दा + म

Verbs	दा 3cU –Irregular Gana-Parasmaipada Chart		
Person	Singular	Dual	Plural
3rd	अददात्	अदत्ताम्	अददुः
2nd	अददाः	अदत्तम्	अदत्त
1st	अददाम्	अदद्व	अदद्म

Sentences using Verbs made from दा दाने 3cU = to give

Sentences	दा 3cU –Irregular Gana-Parasmaipada Chart		
Person	Singular	Dual	Plural
3rd	सः अददात् । He gave.	तौ अदत्ताम् । They both gave.	ते अददुः । They gave.
2nd	त्वं अददाः । You gave.	युवाम् अदत्तम् । You two gave.	यूयम् अदत्त । You gave.
1st	अहं अददाम् । I gave.	आवां अदद्व । We both gave.	वयं अदद्म । We gave.

Root+Affix	दा 3cU – Irregular Gana - Atmanepada Chart		
Person	Singular	Dual	Plural
3rd	अ + दा + त	अ + दा + आताम्	अ + दा + अत
2nd	अ + दा + थाः	अ+ दा + आथाम्	अ + दा + ध्वम्
1st	अ + दा + इ	अ+ दा + वहि	अ + दा + महि

Verbs	दा 3cU – Irregular Gana - Atmanepada Chart		
Person	Singular	Dual	Plural
3rd	अदत्त	अददाताम्	अददत
2nd	अदत्थाः	अददाथाम्	अददध्वम्
1st	अददि	अदद्वहि	अदद्महि

Verb Conjugation Matrix शम्

Imperfect Past Tense Active Voice Verbs लङ् कर्त्तरि प्रयोगः क्रियापदानि

Verbs	शम् 4cP , शाम्य Anga ready for Conjugation		
Person	Singular	Dual	Plural
3rd	अशाम्यत्	अशाम्यताम्	अशाम्यन्
2nd	अशाम्यः	अशाम्यतम्	अशाम्यत
1st	अशाम्यम्	अशाम्याव	अशाम्याम

Verb Conjugation Matrix कृ करणे 8cU = to do

Imperfect Past Tense Active Voice Verbs लङ् कर्त्तरि प्रयोगः क्रियापदानि

Verbs	कृ 8cU -Irregular Gana -Parasmaipada Chart		
Person	Singular	Dual	Plural
3rd	अकरोत्	अकुरुताम्	अकुर्वन्
2nd	अकरो:	अकुरुतम्	अकुरुत
1st	अकरवम्	अकुर्व	अकुर्म

Root+Affix	कृ 8cU - Irregular Gana - Atmanepada Chart		
Person	Singular	Dual	Plural
3rd	अ + कृ + त	अ + कृ + आताम्	अ + कृ + अत
2nd	अ + कृ + था:	अ+ कृ + आथाम्	अ + कृ + ध्वम्
1st	अ + कृ + इ	अ+ कृ + वहि	अ + कृ + महि

Verbs	कृ 8cU - Irregular Gana - Atmanepada Chart		
Person	Singular	Dual	Plural
3rd	अकुरुत	अकुर्वाताम्	अकुर्वत
2nd	अकुरुथा:	अकुर्वाथाम्	अकुरुध्वम्
1st	अकुर्वि	अकुर्वहि	अकुर्महि

Aorist Past Tense

लुङ् = Past tense from now and before that. Past Tense that captures the moment bygone. In a fraction of a second it is past. Why worry?

Let go, Drop, Move on.

This is a favorite tense used in the Upanishads and the Bhagavad Gita. It is used specifically to alleviate the trauma of hardships and difficult times. When our citta becomes clear, when the mind regains its poise, Life becomes Beautiful.

This tense has 12 sets of affixes, i.e. 7x9 sets in Parasmaipada and 5x9 sets in Atmanepada. Some sets affix to only सेट् Roots, others to अनिट् Roots. Sample Verbs listed.

Verbs	भू 1cP = to be, to exist		
Person	Singular	Dual	Plural
3rd	अभूत्	अभूताम्	अभूवन्
2nd	अभू:	अभूतम्	अभूत
1st	अभूवम्	अभूव	अभूम

Verbs	लभ् 1cA = to get		
Person	Singular	Dual	Plural
3rd	अलब्ध	अलप्साताम्	अलप्सत
2nd	अलब्धा:	अलप्साथाम्	अलब्ध्वम्
1st	अलप्सि	अलप्स्वहि	अलप्स्महि

Verbs	दा 3cU – Irregular Gana = to give, to donate					
	Parasmaipada Chart			Atmanepada Chart		
Person	Singular	Dual	Plural	Singular	Dual	Plural
3rd	अदात्	अदाताम्	अदु:	अदित	अदिषाताम्	अदिषत
2nd	अदा:	अदातम्	अदात	अदिथा:	अदिषाथाम्	अदिढ्वम्
1st	अदाम्	अदाव	अदाम	अदिषि	अदिष्वहि	अदिष्महि

Verbs	शम् 4cP		
Person	Singular	Dual	Plural
3rd	अशमत्	अशमताम्	अशमन्
2nd	अशम:	अशमतम्	अशमत
1st	अशमम्	अशमाव	अशमाम

Verbs	कृ 8cU – Irregular Gana = to do, to make					
	Parasmaipada Chart			Atmanepada Chart		
Person	Singular	Dual	Plural	Singular	Dual	Plural
3rd	अकार्षीत्	अकार्ष्टम्	अकार्षु:	अकृत	अकृषाताम्	अकृषत
2nd	अकार्षी:	अकार्ष्टम्	अकार्ष्ट	अकृथा:	अकृषाथाम्	अकृढ्वम्
1st	अकार्षम्	अकार्ष्व	अकार्ष्म	अकृषि	अकृष्वहि	अकृष्महि

Distant Past Tense

लिट् = Perfect Past Tense. Past tense beyond one's birth. Beyond anyone's reach. A past tense that began with TIME, that can only be theorized. A past so distant that no living mortal hath witnessed it.

This is the Beauty of Sanskrit. The great seers spoke of events that were whispered to them by the Supreme Consciousness. Events that were directly bespoken by Brahman.

Sample Verbs listed, this tense is not in use in modern times.

Verbs	भू 1cP – लिट् Distant Past Tense		
Person	Singular	Dual	Plural
3rd	बभूव	बभूवतुः	बभूवुः
2nd	बभूविथ	बभूवथुः	बभूव
1st	बभूव	बभूविव	बभूविम

Verbs	लभ् 1cA – लिट् Distant Past Tense		
Person	Singular	Dual	Plural
3rd	लेभे	लेभाते	लेभिरे
2nd	लेभिषे	लेभाथे	लेभिध्वे
1st	लेभे	लेभिवहे	लेभिमहे

Verbs	दा 3cU – लिट् Distant Past Tense					
	Parasmaipada Chart			Atmanepada Chart		
Person	Singular	Dual	Plural	Singular	Dual	Plural
3rd	ददौ	ददतुः	ददुः	ददे	ददाते	ददिरे
2nd	ददाथ , ददिथ	ददथुः	दद	ददिषे	ददाथे	ददिध्वे
1st	ददौ	ददिव	ददिम	ददे	ददिवहे	ददिमहे

Verbs	शम् 4cP – लिट् Distant Past Tense		
Person	Singular	Dual	Plural
3rd	शशाम	शेमतुः	शेमुः
2nd	शेमिथ	शेमथुः	शेम
1st	शशाम , शशम	शेमिव	शेमिम

Verbs	कृ 8cU – लिट् Distant Past Tense					
	Parasmaipada Chart			Atmanepada Chart		
Person	Singular	Dual	Plural	Singular	Dual	Plural
3rd	चकार	चक्रतुः	चक्रुः	चक्रे	चक्राते	चक्रिरे
2nd	चकर्थ	चक्रथुः	चक्र	चकृषे	चक्राथे	चकृढ्वे
1st	चकार , चकर	चकृव	चकृम	चक्रे	चकृवहे	चकृमहे

Future Tense

Simple Future Tense लृट् Now Onwards

Very easy to conjugate, we simply follow
- the conjugation procedure of Present Tense लट् ,
- with the Vikarana स्य, (by Sandhi it may become ष्य)
- and using the इदित् attribute of Roots.

Verbs	भू 1cP – लृट् Simple Future Tense		
Person	Singular	Dual	Plural
3rd	भविष्यति	भविष्यतः	भविष्यन्ति
2nd	भविष्यसि	भविष्यथः	भविष्यथ
1st	भविष्यामि	भविष्यावः	भविष्यामः

Verbs	लभ् 1cA – लृट् Simple Future Tense		
Person	Singular	Dual	Plural
3rd	लप्स्यते	लप्स्येते	लप्स्यन्ते
2nd	लप्स्यसे	लप्स्येथे	लप्स्यध्वे
1st	लप्स्ये	लप्स्यावहे	लप्स्यामहे

Verbs	दा 3cU – लृट् Simple Future Tense					
	Parasmaipada Chart			Atmanepada Chart		
Person	Singular	Dual	Plural	Singular	Dual	Plural
3rd	दास्यति	दास्यतः	दास्यन्ति	दास्यते	दास्येते	दास्यन्ते
2nd	दास्यसि	दास्यथः	दास्यथ	दास्यसे	दास्येथे	दास्यध्वे
1st	दास्यामि	दास्यावः	दास्यामः	दास्ये	दास्यावहे	दास्यामहे

Verbs	शम् 4cP – लृट् Simple Future Tense		
Person	Singular	Dual	Plural
3rd	शमिष्यति	शमिष्यतः	शमिष्यन्ति
2nd	शमिष्यसि	शमिष्यथः	शमिष्यथ
1st	शमिष्यामि	शमिष्यावः	शमिष्यामः

Verbs	कृ 8cU – लृट् Simple Future Tense					
	Parasmaipada Chart			Atmanepada Chart		
Person	Singular	Dual	Plural	Singular	Dual	Plural
3rd	करिष्यति	करिष्यतः	करिष्यन्ति	करिष्यते	करिष्येते	करिष्यन्ते
2nd	करिष्यसि	करिष्यथः	करिष्यथ	करिष्यसे	करिष्येथे	करिष्यध्वे
1st	करिष्यामि	करिष्यावः	करिष्यामः	करिष्ये	करिष्यावहे	करिष्यामहे

Periphrastic Future Tense लुट् Tomorrow onwards

Sample Verbs listed, this tense is not in use in modern times.

Verbs	भू 1cP – लुट् Periphrastic Future Tense		
Person	Singular	Dual	Plural
3rd	भविता	भवितारौ	भवितारः
2nd	भवितासि	भवितास्थः	भवितास्थ
1st	भवितास्मि	भवितास्वः	भवितास्मः

Verbs	लभ् 1cA – लुट् Periphrastic Future Tense		
Person	Singular	Dual	Plural
3rd	लब्धा	लब्धारौ	लब्धारः
2nd	लब्धासे	लब्धासाथे	लब्धाध्वे
1st	लब्धाहे	लब्धास्वहे	लब्धास्महे

Verbs	दा 3cU – लुट् Periphrastic Future Tense					
	Parasmaipada Chart			Atmanepada Chart		
Person	Singular	Dual	Plural	Singular	Dual	Plural
3rd	दाता	दातारौ	दातारः	दाता	दातारौ	दातारः
2nd	दातासि	दातास्थः	दातास्थ	दातासे	दातासाथे	दाताध्वे

| 1st | दातास्मि | दातास्वः | दातास्मः | दाताहे | दातास्वहे | दातास्महे |

Verbs	शम् 4cP – लुट् Periphrastic Future Tense		
Person	Singular	Dual	Plural
3rd	शमिता	शमितारौ	शमितारः
2nd	शमितासि	शमितास्थः	शमितास्थ
1st	शमितास्मि	शमितास्वः	शमितास्मः

Verbs	कृ 8cU – लुट् Periphrastic Future Tense					
	Parasmaipada Chart			Atmanepada Chart		
Person	Singular	Dual	Plural	Singular	Dual	Plural
3rd	कर्ता	कर्तारौ	कर्तारः	कर्ता	कर्तारौ	कर्तारः
2nd	कर्तासि	कर्तास्थः	कर्तास्थ	कर्तासे	कर्तासाथे	कर्ताध्वे
1st	कर्तास्मि	कर्तास्वः	कर्तास्मः	कर्ताहे	कर्तास्वहे	कर्तास्महे

Conditional Mood लृङ् – If/Then in Past or Future sense

Very easy to conjugate, we simply follow
- the conjugation procedure of Imperfect Past Tense लङ् ,
- with the Vikarana स्य, (by Sandhi it may become ष्य)
- and using the इदित् attribute of Roots.

Verbs	भू 1cP – लृङ् Conditional Mood		
Person	Singular	Dual	Plural
3rd	अभविष्यत्	अभविष्यताम्	अभविष्यन्
2nd	अभविष्यः	अभविष्यतम्	अभविष्यत
1st	अभविष्यम्	अभविष्याव	अभविष्याम

Verbs	लभ् 1cA – लृङ् Conditional Mood		
Person	Singular	Dual	Plural
3rd	अलप्स्यत	अलप्स्येताम्	अलप्स्यन्त
2nd	अलप्स्यथाः	अलप्स्येथाम्	अलप्स्यध्वम्
1st	अलप्स्ये	अलप्स्यावहि	अलप्स्यामहि

Verbs	दा 3cU – लृङ् Conditional Mood					
	Parasmaipada Chart			Atmanepada Chart		
Person	Singular	Dual	Plural	Singular	Dual	Plural
3rd	अदास्यत्	अदास्यताम्	अदास्यन्	अदास्यत	अदास्येताम्	अदास्यन्त
2nd	अदास्यः	अदास्यतम्	अदास्यत	अदास्यथाः	अदास्येथाम्	अदास्यध्वम्
1st	अदास्यम्	अदास्याव	अदास्याम	अदास्ये	अदास्यावहि	अदास्यामहि

Verbs	शम् 4cP – लृङ् Conditional Mood		
Person	Singular	Dual	Plural
3rd	अशमिष्यत्	अशमिष्यताम्	अशमिष्यन्
2nd	अशमिष्यः	अशमिष्यतम्	अशमिष्यत
1st	अशमिष्यम्	अशमिष्याव	अशमिष्याम

Verbs	कृ 8cU – लृङ् Conditional Mood					
	Parasmaipada Chart			Atmanepada Chart		
Person	Singular	Dual	Plural	Singular	Dual	Plural
3rd	अकरिष्यत्	अकरिष्यताम्	अकरिष्यन्	अकरिष्यत	अकरिष्यत	अकरिष्यत
2nd	अकरिष्यः	अकरिष्यतम्	अकरिष्यत	अकरिष्यत	अकरिष्यत	अकरिष्यत
1st	अकरिष्यम्	अकरिष्याव	अकरिष्याम	अकरिष्यत	अकरिष्यत	अकरिष्यत
If it rains I cannot make it. यदा अवर्षिष्यत् तदा अहं न अकरिष्यम् ।						

Imperative Mood लोट् – A gentle request

This is frequently seen in Sanskrit literature. Easy to conjugate, its Ting affixes are like Imperfect Past Tense लङ् with few changes

Verbs	भू 1cP , लोट् Imperative Mood "let it be"		
Person	Singular	Dual	Plural
3rd	भवतु , भवतात्	भवताम्	भवन्तु
2nd	भव , भवतात्	भवतम्	भवत
1st	भवानि	भवाव	भवाम

Verbs	लभ् 1cA , लोट् Imperative Mood "may get"		
Person	Singular	Dual	Plural
3rd	लभताम्	लभेताम्	लभन्ताम्
2nd	लभस्व	लभेथाम्	लभध्वम्
1st	लभै	लभावहै	लभामहै

Verbs	दा 3cU – लोट् Imperative Mood "may give"					
	Parasmaipada Chart			Atmanepada Chart		
Person	Singular	Dual	Plural	Singular	Dual	Plural
3rd	ददातु , दत्तात्	दत्ताम्	ददतु	दत्ताम्	ददाताम्	ददताम्
2nd	देहि , दत्तात्	दत्तम्	दत्त	दत्स्व	ददाथाम्	ददध्वम्
1st	ददानि	ददाव	ददाम	ददै	ददावहै	ददामहै

Verbs	शम् 4cP , लोट् Imperative Mood "please be calm"		
Person	Singular	Dual	Plural
3rd	शाम्यतु, शाम्यतात्	शाम्यताम्	शाम्यन्तु
2nd	शाम्य , शाम्यतात्	शाम्यतम्	शाम्यत
1st	शाम्यानि	शाम्याव	शाम्याम

Verbs	कृ 8cU – लोट् Imperative Mood "please do"					
	Parasmaipada Chart			Atmanepada Chart		
Person	Singular	Dual	Plural	Singular	Dual	Plural
3rd	करोतु , कुरुतात्	कुरुताम्	कुर्वन्तु	कुरुताम्	कुर्वाताम्	कुर्वताम्
2nd	कुरु , कुरुतात्	कुरुतम्	कुरुत	कुरुष्व	कुर्वाथाम्	कुरुध्वम्
1st	करवाणि	करवाव	करवाम	करवै	करवावहै	करवामहै

Potential Mood विधिलिङ् – An order

This is frequently seen in the Bhagavad Gita, and I'm sure we all use it in our classrooms, albeit in our own tongue. Easy to conjugate.

Verbs	भू 1cP , विधिलिङ् Potential Mood "must be"		
Person	Singular	Dual	Plural
3rd	भवेत्	भवेताम्	भवेयुः
2nd	भवेः	भवेतम्	भवेत
1st	भवेयम्	भवेव	भवेम

Verbs	लभ् 1cA,विधिलिङ् Potential Mood "should get"		
Person	Singular	Dual	Plural
3rd	लभेत	लभेयाताम्	लभेरन्
2nd	लभेथाः	लभेयाथाम्	लभेध्वम्
1st	लभेय	लभेवहि	लभेमहि

Verbs	दा 3cU – विधिलिङ् Potential Mood "should give"					
	Parasmaipada Chart			Atmanepada Chart		
Person	Singular	Dual	Plural	Singular	Dual	Plural
3rd	दद्यात्	दद्याताम्	दद्युः	ददीत	ददीयाताम्	ददीरन्
2nd	दद्याः	दद्यातम्	दद्यात	ददीथाः	ददीयाथाम्	ददीध्वम्
1st	दद्याम्	दद्याव	दद्याम	ददीय	ददीवहि	ददीमहि

Verbs	शम् 4cP, विधिलिङ् Potential Mood "should be calm"		
Person	Singular	Dual	Plural
3rd	शाम्येत्	शाम्येताम्	शाम्येयुः
2nd	शाम्येः	शाम्येतम्	शाम्येत
1st	शाम्येयम्	शाम्येव	शाम्येम

Verbs	कृ 8cU – विधिलिङ् Potential Mood "must do"					
	Parasmaipada Chart			Atmanepada Chart		
Person	Singular	Dual	Plural	Singular	Dual	Plural
3rd	कुर्यात्	कुर्याताम्	कुर्युः	कुर्वीत	कुर्वीयाताम्	कुर्वीरन्
2nd	कुर्याः	कुर्यातम्	कुर्यात	कुर्वीथाः	कुर्वीयाथाम्	कुर्वीध्वम्
1st	कुर्याम्	कुर्याव	कुर्याम	कुर्वीय	कुर्वीवहि	कुर्वीमहि

Benedictive Mood आशीर् लिङ्– Blessing or curse

This is frequently seen in the Vedas and Upanishads.

Verbs	भू 1cP, आशीर्लिङ् Benedictive Mood "be blessed"		
Person	Singular	Dual	Plural
3rd	भूयात्	भूयास्ताम्	भूयासुः
2nd	भूयाः	भूयास्तम्	भूयास्त
1st	भूयासम्	भूयास्व	भूयास्म

Verbs	लभ् 1cA, आशीर्लिङ् Benedictive Mood		
Person	Singular	Dual	Plural
3rd	लप्सीष्ट	लप्सीयास्ताम्	लप्सीरन्
2nd	लप्सीष्ठाः	लप्सीयास्थाम्	लप्सीध्वम्
1st	लप्सीय	लप्सीवहि	लप्सीमहि

दा 3cU	Parasmaipada Chart			Atmanepada Chart		
Person	Singular	Dual	Plural	Singular	Dual	Plural
3rd	देयात्	देयास्ताम्	देयासुः	दासीष्ट	दासीयास्ताम्	दासीरन्
2nd	देयाः	देयास्तम्	देयास्त	दासीष्ठाः	दासीयास्थाम्	दासीध्वम्
1st	देयासम्	देयास्व	देयास्म	दासीय	दासीवहि	दासीमहि

Verbs	शम् 4cP, आशीर्लिङ् Benedictive Mood		
Person	Singular	Dual	Plural
3rd	शम्यात्	शम्यास्ताम्	शम्यासुः
2nd	शम्याः	शम्यास्तम्	शम्यास्त
1st	शम्यासम्	शम्यास्व	शम्यास्म

कृ 8cU	Parasmaipada Chart			Atmanepada Chart		
Person	Singular	Dual	Plural	Singular	Dual	Plural
3rd	क्रियात्	क्रियास्ताम्	क्रियासुः	कृषीष्ट	कृषीयास्ताम्	कृषीरन्
2nd	क्रियाः	क्रियास्तम्	क्रियास्त	कृषीष्ठाः	कृषीयास्थाम्	कृषीध्वम्
1st	क्रियासम्	क्रियास्व	क्रियास्म	कृषीय	कृषीवहि	कृषीमहि

Additional Senses of Verbs

Passive Tense यक् - Reported

Passive voice is used when reporting is done. Active voice is used when an event is happening in real time, and when the same event is reported, then the passive voice is used.

भाव–कर्मणो: ।
In Sanskrit, we have the concept of Passive Voice कर्मणि प्रयोग: and the additional concept of Internal Voice भावे प्रयोग: , that can be loosely translated as "the sense of the action".

So we have Verbs in the three Voices, namely
कर्त्तरि प्रयोग: Active Voice = an action being done.
कर्मणि प्रयोग: Passive Voice = an action being reported.
भावे प्रयोग: Internal Voice = the sense of the action, rather than the action itself. Such usage is not prevalent in English, so we cannot make apt translations.

To make Verbs, we apply Ting Affixes to the Roots. This is the standard procedure for Active Voice. To make Verbs in Passive Voice, an additional Affix, the यक् प्रत्यय: is inserted in the process prior to the तिङ् प्रत्यय: Ting Affix.

In case of the भावे प्रयोग: Internal Voice, the procedure is identical to the procedure for the कर्मणि प्रयोग: Passive Voice, with a notable difference that भावे Verbs will only be conjugated in third person singular. It means that there is no matrix, just one Verb per Root in Internal Voice . Another key difference lies not in the procedure of Verb formation, but in the Root itself that is to be conjugated.

The Roots in the Dhatupatha those have the attribute of सकर्मक: धातु: Transitive Root, can be used in the sense of Passive Voice. Whereas the Roots in the Dhatupatha those have the attribute of

अकर्मकः धातुः Intransitive Root, can be used in the sense of Internal Voice. This attribute सकर्मकः / अकर्मकः is not stated in standard Dhatupathas. However it is given in Dhatupatha commentaries.

Transitive Roots are those whose Verbs can be associated with a physical object. Intransitive Roots are those for which there isn't a physical object to frame sentences using their Verbs.

In Sanskrit, the Verbs made from Transitive Roots can be used in Active Voice and Passive Voice in different sentences. Verbs made from Intransitive Roots can be used in Active Voice and Internal Voice in different sentences.

Verbs using Roots भू 1cP, पठ् 1cP, लभ् 1cA, दा 3cU, शम् 4cP, कृ 8cU

Active Voice कर्त्तरि प्रयोगः	भू	1cP	अकर्मकः	कर्त्तरि	सः भवति । He is.	
	पठ्	1cP	सकर्मकः	कर्त्तरि	सः शाम्यति । He is calm.	
	लभ्	1cA	सकर्मकः	कर्त्तरि	सः लभते । He gets.	
	दा	3cU	सकर्मकः	कर्त्तरि	सः ददाति । He gives.	सः दत्ते । He gives.
	शम्	4cP	अकर्मकः	कर्त्तरि	सः पठति । He reads.	
	कृ	8cU	सकर्मकः	कर्त्तरि	सः करोति । He does.	सः कुरुते । He does.
Internal Voice भावे प्रयोगः	भू	1cP	अकर्मकः	भावे	तेन भूयते ।	
	शम्	4cP	अकर्मकः	भावे	तेन शम्यते ।	
Passive Voice कर्मणि प्रयोगः	पठ्	1cP	सकर्मकः	कर्मणि	तत् तेन पठ्यते । It is read by him.	
	लभ्	1cP	सकर्मकः	कर्मणि	तत् तेन लभ्यते । It is received by him.	
	दा	3cP	सकर्मकः	कर्मणि	तत् तेन दीयते । It is given by him.	
	कृ	8cU	सकर्मकः	कर्मणि	तत् तेन क्रियते । It is done by him.	

Now we see the charts for the Passive Voice. This has the peculiarity that for all the Roots, whether they are listed as Parasmaipada or Atmanepada in the Dhatupatha, we shall apply only Atmanepada Ting Affixes in Passive Voice.

Present Tense Passive Voice Chart without Tag letters -
Regular Ganas 1c, 4c, 6c, 10c. लट् कर्मणि प्रयोगः

तिङ् प्रत्ययः	Whether "Parasmaipadi" or "Atmanepadi" Roots, all use Atmanepada affixes only in Passive Voice		
Person	Singular	Dual	Plural
3rd	य + ते	य + इते	य + अन्ते
2nd	य + से	य + इथे	य + ध्वे
1st	य + ए	य + वहे	य + महे

Present Tense Passive Voice Chart without Tag letters
irRegular Ganas 2c, 3c, 5c, 7c, 8c, 9c. लट् कर्मणि प्रयोगः

तिङ् प्रत्ययः	Whether "Parasmaipadi" or "Atmanepadi" Roots, all use Atmanepada affixes only in Passive Voice		
Person	Singular	Dual	Plural
3rd	य + ते	य + आते	य + अते * (अति for the 3c group)
2nd	य + से	य + आथे	य + ध्वे
1st	य + ए	य + वहे	य + महे

Present Tense Passive Voice Chart without Tag letters
Modified by an Ashtadhyayi Sutra
Regular Ganas 1c, 4c, 6c, 10c. लट् कर्मणि प्रयोगः

तिङ् प्रत्ययः	Whether "Parasmaipadi" or "Atmanepadi" Roots, all use Atmanepada affixes only in Passive Voice		
Person	Singular	Dual	Plural
3rd	य + ते	य + इते	यू + अन्ते
2nd	य + से	य + इथे	य + ध्वे
1st	यू + ए	य + आवहे	य + आमहे

Present Tense Passive Voice Chart without Tag letters
Modified by an Ashtadhyayi Sutra
irRegular Ganas 2c, 3c, 5c, 7c, 8c, 9c. लट् कर्मणि प्रयोगः

तिङ् प्रत्ययः	Whether "Parasmaipadi" or "Atmanepadi" Roots, all use Atmanepada affixes only in Passive Voice		
Person	Singular	Dual	Plural
3rd	य + ते	य + आते	य् + अते * (अति for the 3c group)
2nd	य + से	य + आथे	य + ध्वे
1st	य् + ए	य + आवहे	य + आमहे

Desiderative सन् – Desiring

See दा 3cU = to give. दीत्सति । He desires to give.

Causative णिच् – Impelling

The sanadi affix णिच् is applied for two purposes. It is applied for Roots of the 10c Conjugational Group, and there it does not alter the meaning of the Root. So after the 10c Roots, the णिच् affix is not causal, it does not impel. However, when the णिच् affix is applied to any Root not belonging to 10c, then it signifies a causal action, inspiring someone else to act. E.g. सः गच्छति । He goes. सः गमयति । He impels (someone) to go. अहं पठामि । I study. अहं पाठयामि । I impel (someone) to study. भू भावयति He impels to be. । कृ कारयति । He impels to perform. पठ् पाठयति । दा दापयति । Another point to note is that the णिच् affix causes each and every Root to have both Parasmaipada and Atmanepada endings, irrespective of their Dhatupatha listing. Thus गमयति , गमयते । पाठयति , पाठयते । Further, the interesting thing to note is that causal णिच् can also be applied to 10c conjugational group, after the simple णिच् has already been applied. Thus to make causal verbs from 10c, णिच् is to be applied twice. However due to a grammar rule, the second णिच् gets dropped after making the meaning causal, and the final Verb has the same spelling as before. Thus चुर् 10c चोरयति , चोरयते । He steals. And चोरयति , चोरयते । He makes someone steal.

Repetitive यङ् – Frequently doing or Intensely

The sanadi affix यङ् is applied for few Roots only. It signifies the action being done again and again. It is also used in the sense of Intense action. It is not applied in presence of Upasarga. It will take only Atmanepada Ting Affixes during Verb formation due to the presence of ङ् Tag letter.

Elision of Repetitive affix यङ् लुक्

When applied to certain Roots, the यङ् affix gets elided. लुक् means elision, so when यङ् affix is applied but dropped entirely and is not visible in the final word, the process is called यङ्लुक् । In this case the Roots will take Parasmaipada or Atmanepada affixes as per Root attribute. Meaning of the word remains same, i.e. Repetitive or Intensive action.

Denominative क्रिप् – Meaning follows Noun Stem

When certain Sanadi Affixes are applied to प्रातिपदिक Stems, the result is a new Secondary Root. Then by adding Ting Affixes, Verbs are made. The meaning of these Verbs will reflect the meaning of the प्रातिपदिक Stem.

Verb Matrix Summary for पठ् 1cP – to study

The Root पठ व्यक्तायां वाचि of 1c is परस्मैपदी , सेट् , सकर्मक धातुः ।

लट् कर्त्तरि PresentTense ActiveVoice			लङ् Imperfect Past Tense		
पठति	पठतः	पठन्ति	अपठत्	अपठताम्	अपठन्
पठसि	पठथः	पठथ	अपठः	अपठतम्	अपठत
पठामि	पठावः	पठामः	अपठम्	अपठाव	अपठाम

पठ् 1cP, लोट् Imperative Mood			विधिलिङ् Potential Mood		
पठतु, –तात्	पठताम्	पठन्तु	पठेत्	पठेताम्	पठेयुः
पठ , –तात्	पठतम्	पठत	पठेः	पठेतम्	पठेत
पठानि	पठाव	पठाम	पठेयम्	पठेव	पठेम

लृट् Simple Future Tense			लुट् Periphrastic Future Tense		
पठिष्यति	पठिष्यतः	पठिष्यन्ति	पठिता	पठितारौ	पठितारः
पठिष्यसि	पठिष्यथः	पठिष्यथ	पठितासि	पठितास्थः	पठितास्थ
पठिष्यामि	पठिष्यावः	पठायामः	पठितास्मि	पठितास्वः	पठितास्मः

लुङ् Aorist Past Tense (one set)			लिट् Distant Past Tense		
अपठीत्	अपठिष्टाम्	अपठन्ति	पपाठ	पेठतुः	पेठुः
अपठीः	अपठिष्टम्	अपठिष्ट	पेठिथ	पेठथुः	पेठ
अपठिषम्	अपठिष्व	अपठिष्म	पपाठ,पपठ	पेठिव	पेठिम

लृङ् Conditional Mood			आशीर्लिङ् Benedictive Mood		
अपठिष्यत्	अपठिष्यताम्	अपठिष्यन्	पठ्यात्	पठ्यास्ताम्	पठ्यासुः
अपठिष्यः	अपठिष्यतम्	अपठिष्यत	पठ्याः	पठ्यास्तम्	पठ्यास्त
अपठिष्यम्	अपठिष्याव	अपठिष्याम	पठ्यासम्	पठ्यास्व	पठ्यास्म

लट् कर्मणि Present Tense Passive Voice. यक् + Atmanepada Affix			लङ् कर्मणि Imperfect Past Tense Passive Voice. यक् + Atmane		
पठ्यते	पठ्येते	पठ्यन्ते	अपठ्यत	अपठ्येताम्	अपठ्यन्त
पठ्यसे	पठ्येथे	पठ्यध्वे	अपठ्यथाः	अपठ्येथाम्	अपठ्यध्वम्
पठ्ये	पठ्यावहे	पठ्यामहे	अपठ्ये	अपठ्यावहि	अपठ्यामहि

सन् लट् Desiderative Present Tense. सन् + तिङ् Parasmaipada " to desire to study"			सन् लङ् Desiderative Imperfect Past Tense. सन् + तिङ् Parasmaipada "desired to study"		
पिपठिषति	पिपठिषतः	पिपठिषन्ति	अपिपठिषत्	अपिपठिषताम्	अपिपठिषन्
पिपठिषसि	पिपठिषथः	पिपठिषथ	अपिपठिषः	अपिपठिषतम्	अपिपठिषत
पिपठिषामि	पिपठिषावः	पिपठिषामः	अपिपठिषम्	अपिपठिषाव	अपिपठिषाम

णिच् लट् Causal Present Tense. णिच् + तिङ् Parasmaipada " to impel someone to study"	णिच् लङ् Causal Imperfect Past Tense. णिच् + तिङ् Parasmaipada "impelled someone to study"

पाठयति	पाठयतः	पाठयन्ति	अपाठयत्	अपाठयताम्	अपाठयन्
पाठयसि	पाठयथः	पाठयथ	अपाठयः	अपाठयतम्	अपाठयत
पाठयामि	पाठयावः	पाठयामः	अपाठयम्	अपाठयाव	अपाठयाम

णिच् लट् Causal Present Tense. णिच् + तिङ् Atmanepada " to impel someone to study"			णिच् लङ् Causal Imperfect Past Tense. णिच् + तिङ् Atmanepada "impelled someone to study"		
पाठयते	पाठयेते	पाठयन्ते	अपाठयत	अपाठयेताम्	अपाठयन्त
पाठयसे	पाठयेथे	पाठयध्वे	अपाठयथाः	अपाठयेथाम्	अपाठयध्वम्
पाठये	पाठयावहे	पाठयामहे	अपाठये	अपाठयावहि	अपाठयामहि

यङ् लट् RepetitivePresentTense यङ् + तिङ् Atmanepada " to study again and again" or "to study earnestly"			यङ् लङ् Repetitive Imperfect Past Tense. यङ् + तिङ् Atmanepada "studied again and again" or "studied earnestly"		
पापठ्यते	पापठ्येते	पापठ्यन्ते	अपापठ्यत	अपापठ्येताम्	अपापठ्यन्त
पापठ्यसे	पापठ्येथे	पापठ्यध्वे	अपापठ्यथाः	अपापठ्येथाम्	अपापठ्यध्वम्
पापठ्ये	पापठ्यावहे	पापठ्यामहे	अपापठ्ये	अपापठ्यावहि	अपापठ्यामहि

दा – यङ् – Repetitive – देदीयते । Gives Again and Again. Gives Earnestly. दा – यङ्लुक् – Repetitive – दादेति , दादाति । Gives Again and Again. Gives Earnestly. (for पठ् an entry was not found).

Nouns that serve as Verbs, made using Krit Affixes.

पठ् – शतृ – Parasmaipada Root Present Participle पठत् – पठन् m1/1 , पठन्ती f1/1 , पठत् n1/1 । reading, studying, learning.

(since the alternate present participle affix शानच् is only used for Atmanepadi Roots, we give the example for Root दा 3cU).

दा – शतृ – Parasmaipada Root Present Participle ददत् – ददन् m1/1 , ददन्ती f1/1 , ददत् n1/1 । giving.

दा – शानच् – Atmanepada Root Present Participle ददान – ददानः m1/1 , ददानी f1/1 , ददानम् n1/1 । giving.

पठ् – क्तवत् – Active Past Participle पठितवत् – पठितवान् m1/1 , पठितवती f1/1 , पठितवत् n1/1 । was Read, was Studied, was Learnt.

पठ् – क्त – Passive Past Participle पठित – पठितः m1/1 , पठिता f1/1 , पठितम् n1/1 । Read, Studied, Learnt.

पठ् – तुमुन् – Infinitive पठितुम् । Indeclinable - to read.

पठ् – क्त्वा – Gerund पठित्वा । Indeclinable - having read.

प्र+पठ् – ल्यप् – Gerund प्रपठ्य । Indeclinable - specially having read.

पठ् – य – Gerundive पाठ्य – पाठ्यः m1/1 , पाठ्या f1/1 , पाठ्यम् n1/1 । ought to be read.

पठ् – तव्यत् – Gerundive पठितव्य – पठितव्यः m1/1 , पठितव्या f1/1 , पठितव्यम् n1/1 । ought to be read.

पठ् – अनीयर् – Gerundive पठनीय – पठनीयः m1/1 , पठनीया f1/1 , पठनीयम् n1/1 । ought to be read.

पठ् – ल्युट् – "sense of Root" पठन । पठनम् n1/1 । Neuter Gender only – to read.

Kridantas

The कृत् प्रत्यय Krit affix is famous for making प्रातिपदिक stems that go on to make Nouns. Since these stems are made using the Krit Affixes, another name for these stems is कृदन्त kridanta i.e. Krit-ending. Apart from Nouns, some words made from the Kridantas function as Verbs. Such words are named Participles. Since they are technically nouns, so they shall decline in a 7x3 matrix. The most famous of these participles is the Passive Past Participle, made using the क्त affix.

Active and Passive Past Participles

Some frequently used participles are the(PPP) passive past and (PPA) active past, known as nishtha निष्ठा ।

Boys with a ball played.

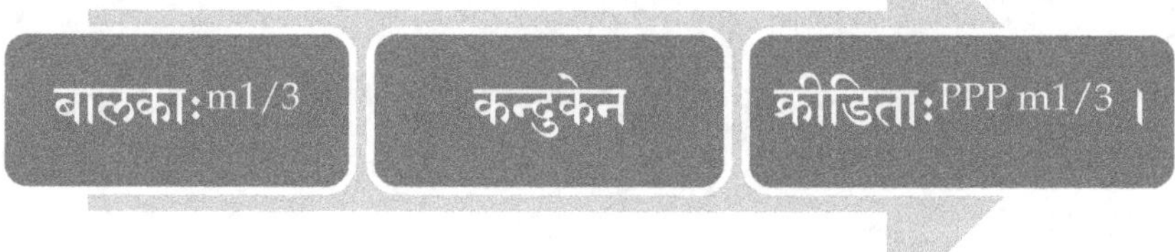

Krit Affixes to make other Verbs

Present Participles "doing" sense शतृ or शानच्
Past Participles "past tense" sense क्त or क्तवत्
Infinitives "to do" sense तुमुन् Indeclinable

Gerunds "having done" sense क्त्वा or ल्यप् Indeclinable
क्त्वा is added to Roots without Upasarga. Gerunds are also termed
Continuatives since action is still happening.
कृ 8cU + क्त्वा → कृत्वा । stem + सुप् → कृत्वा । Indeclinable
ल्यप् is added to Roots with Upasarga.
प्र + कृ 8cU + ल्यप् → प्रकृत्य । stem + सुप् → प्रकृत्य । Indeclinable

Gerundives "ought to do" "विधि लिङ्" sense तव्यत् तव्य अनीयर्
तव्यत्
भू 1cP + तव्यत् → भवितव्य । stem + सुप् → भवितव्यम् । n1/1
पठ् 1cP + तव्यत् → पठितव्य । stem + सुप् → पठितव्यम् । n1/1
दा 3cU + तव्यत् → दातव्य । stem + सुप् → दातव्यम् । n1/1
कृ 8cU + तव्यत् → कर्तव्य । stem + सुप् → कर्तव्यम् । n1/1

अनीयर्
भू 1cP + अनीयर् → भवितव्य । stem + सुप् → भवितव्यम् । n1/1
पठ् 1cP + अनीयर् → पठनीय । stem + सुप् → पठनीयम् । n1/1
लभ् 1cA + अनीयर् → लभनीय । stem + सुप् → लभनीयम् । n1/1
दा 3cU + अनीयर् → दानीय । stem + सुप् → दानीयम् । n1/1
कृ 8cU + अनीयर् → करणीय । stem + सुप् → करणीयम् । n1/1

Krit Affixes to make common Nouns तृच् ण्वुल् घञ्

पठ् – तृच् – Doer पठितृ । पठिता m1/1 पठित्री f1/1 पठितृ n1/1 । the student.

पठ् – ण्वुल् – Doer पाठक । पाठकः m1/1 पाठिका f1/1 पाठकम् n1/1 । the student. (for practical purposes, a student can be male or female or transgender).

पठ् – घञ् – Object पाठ । पाठः m1/1 पाठा f1/1 पाठम् n1/1 । the lesson.

Noun Attributes
The 7x3 Matrix

Case 1st-2nd-3rd-4th-5th-6th-7th Vocative

Case is also known as Vibhakti, and it lists all the possible situations in which a particular stem can be used in a sentence. This is the inflectional nature of Sanskrit, whereby preposition and exact positional meaning in a sentence is carried within the Noun spelling itself.

Number Singular-Dual-Plural

Any Noun can be described fully in three numbers.
E.g. one brother, twins, many brothers

Gender Masculine-Feminine-Neuter
Nouns in Sanskrit are classified in three genders for the purpose of grammatical declension. Some stems are only declined using masculine affixes, others by using feminine affixes, and some by using neuter affixes. Note that the word "gender" is used here as a grammatical tool since it also applies to words that practically cannot be said to have a masculine or feminine gender, as inanimate objects, or subtle emotions and energies.

Noun Construction Flow Chart

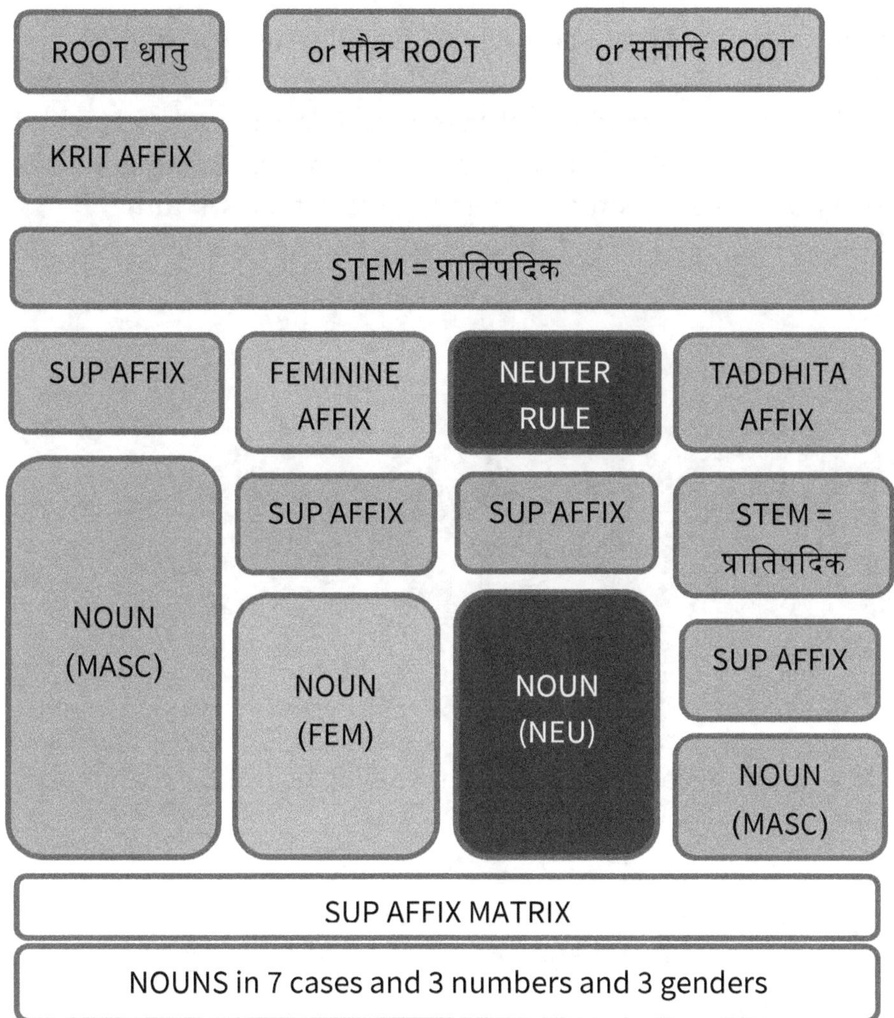

Taddhita तद्धितः = तत् हितः = For its sake, Related to it, etc.
Derived Nouns are easily made beginning with Stems प्रातिपदिकम्
When a Taddhita affix is added to a Stem, it takes on the flavor or
connotation of the original stem, and then the सुप् affix added to it
makes the finished Noun. E.g. stem बुद्धि means "intellect", and the
noun बुद्धिमान् means "the one with a sharp intellect".

बुद्धि stem + मतुप् Taddhita affix → बुद्धिमत् stem →सुप् 1/1 → बुद्धिमान् ।

Anatomy of Noun

Simply put, a solid physical entity or even the subtle matter is called a Noun in grammar. In Sanskrit the word for it is नाम । As we say, this creation is made up of Name and Form, Sound and Light, so in Sanskrit नाम–रूप–प्रपञ्च: इति । नाम = Name. In grammar we see how a Noun gets constructed from the Stem, that is in turn constructed from the Root. All our proper names are Nouns.

Root -> Stem -> Noun. Noun is then ready to be used in a sentence.

Root -> KRit Affix -> Stem. Stems make up the words that are usually used in English literature to specify Sanskrit Nouns.

Stem -> Sup Affix -> Noun. Nouns are the words that are usually used in Sanskrit literature.

Q
Why does English literature use Stems in place of Nouns that are used in Sanskrit Literature?
A
English is an uninflected language, so it is appropriate to use the Stem that has a fixed spelling, since we shall place it with suitable prepositions in a sentence. Sanskrit is an inflected language, so it makes sense to use the correct Noun spelling that can be placed anywhere without preposition in the sentence.

As we shall see, any Noun in Sanskrit has a theoretical count of 21(+3) spelling variations as per usage!

Declension of Nouns

There is the famous सुँप् Affixes table that is used to convert a Stem to a Noun. This table is actually a matrix that builds upon 7 case situations in 3 numbers, known as the 7x3 matrix. Technically 8x3 considering the Vocative case, but that is not for all stems.

Further there is the gender classification, so we have the 7x3 matrix for each of the masculine, feminine and neuter genders.

This means that for stems that can take any gender (e.g. adjectives), we have a total of 7x3x3 = 63 noun spelling variations. A single word can actually have 63 spelling variations in its usage in Sanskrit literature! Theoretical, not a practical reality. However as a student, let's see the matrix.

Situation Case / Number		Singular	Dual	Plural
1	Nominative = Actor or Doer or Protagonist or **Subject**	सुँ	औ	जस्
2	Accusative = **Object**	अम्	औट्	शस्
3	Instrumental = **by, with**	टा	भ्याम्	भिस्
4	Dative = Recipient = **for, to**	ङे	भ्याम्	भ्यस्
5	Ablative = Point-Of-Origin = **from, due to**	ङसि	भ्याम्	भ्यस्
6	Genitive = Possessive = Relationship with another noun = **of**	ङस्	ओस्	आम्
7	Locative = Subject Matter = Place/Time = **in, at, among**	ङि	ओस्	सुँप्
8	Vocative = Hailing someone = Calling aloud the name = **proper nouns only**	संबोधन प्रथमा **same as 1st case**		
		सुँ	औ	जस्

Situation Case / Number		Singular = one entity	Dual = two entities	Plural = three or more
1	Nominative	राम:	रामौ	रामा:
2	Accusative	रामम्	रामौ	रामान्
3	Instrumental	रामेण	रामाभ्याम्	रामै:
4	Dative	रामाय	रामाभ्याम्	रामेभ्य:
5	Ablative	रामात्	रामाभ्याम्	रामेभ्य:
6	Genitive	रामस्य	रामयो:	रामाणाम्
7	Locative	रामे	रामयो:	रामेषु
8	Vocative	With expletive हे		
		हे राम	हे रामौ	हे रामा:

Stem = राम = राम् अ = अकारन्तः पुंलिङ्गः शब्दः । Theoretical Matrix		
	Singular	Dual	Plural
1	रामः पठति ।	रामौ पठतः ।	रामाः पठन्ति ।
	राम reads.	two boys named राम read.	three or more boys named राम read.
2	सीता रामं पश्यति ।	सीता रामौ पश्यति ।	सीता रामान् पश्यति ।
	Sita sees Rāma.	Sita sees two Rāma(s).	Sita sees many Rāma(s).
3	सेना रामेण नीयते ।	सेना रामाभ्यां नीयते ।	सेना रामैः नीयते ।
	Army is led by Rāma.	Army is led by two Rāma(s).	Army is led by many Rāma(s).
4	रामाय नमः ।	रामाभ्यां नमः	रामेभ्यः नमः ।
	Prostration to Rāma.	Prostration to two Rāma(s).	Prostration to many Rāma(s).
5	रामात् शान्तिः उदेति ।	रामाभ्यां शान्तिः उदेति	रामेभ्यः शान्तिः उदेति ।
	Peace arises due to Rāma.	Peace arises due to two Rāma(s).	Peace arises due to many Rāma(s).
6	भरतः रामस्य भ्राता ।	भरतः रामयोः भ्राता ।	भरतः रामाणाम् भ्राता ।
	Bharat is Rāma's brother.	Bharat is brother of two boys named Rāma.	Bharat is brother of many boys named Rāma.
7	श्री राम राम रामेति रमे रामे मनोरमे ।	रामयोः रमे ।	रामेषु रमे ।
	I delight in chanting Rāma.	I delight in two Rāma(s).	I delight in many Rāma(s).
8	हे राम आगच्छ ।	हे रामौ आगच्छतम् ।	हे रामाः आगच्छत ।
	O Rāma! Please come.	O two Rāma(s)! Please come.	O many Rāma(s)! Please come.

Stem = राम = राम् अ = अकारन्तः पुंलिङ्गः शब्दः । Practical Matrix since in real life we may not have all the dual and plural cases.			
Rāma = राम	Singular	Dual	Plural
1	Nominative	रामः पठति ।	रामौ पठतः ।	रामाः पठन्ति ।
		a boy named राम reads	two boys named राम read	three or more boys named राम read
2	Accusative	सीता रामं पश्यति ।	सीता रामौ पश्यति ।	सीता रामान् पश्यति ।
		Sita sees Rāma.	Sita sees two Rāma(s).	Sita sees many Rāma(s).
3	Instrumental	सेना रामेण नीयते ।	x	x
		Army is led by Rāma.		
4	Dative	रामाय नमः ।	x	x
		Prostration to Rāma.		
5	Ablative	रामात् शान्तिः उदेति ।	x	x
		Peace arises due to Rāma.		
6	Genitive	भरतः रामस्य भ्राता ।	x	x
		Bharat is Rāma's brother.		
7	Locative	श्री राम राम रामेति रमे रामे मनोरमे ।	x	x
		I delight in chanting Rāma.		
8	Vocative	हे राम आगच्छ ।	x	x
		O Rāma! Please come.		

Nouns used as Adjectives

The nouns used as adjectives are interesting, because these may decline in any gender to match the substantive in a sentence. E.g.

Adjective	Substantive	Sentence
Good समीचीन	Boy बालकः	समीचीनः बालकः ।
Good समीचीन	Girl बालिका	समीचीना बालिका ।
Good समीचीन	Fruit फलम्	समीचीनं फलम् ।

Noun 7x3 Matrix in 3 genders - with Vocative

राम –अकारान्तः पुंलिङ्गः			दुर्गा – आकारान्तः स्त्रीलिङ्गः			फल – अकारान्तः नपुंसकलिङ्गः		
रामः	रामौ	रामाः	दुर्गा	दुर्गे	दुर्गाः	फलम्	फले	फलानि
रामम्	रामौ	रामान्	दुर्गाम्	दुर्गे	दुर्गाः	फलम्	फले	फलानि
रामेण	रामाभ्यां	रामैः	दुर्गया	दुर्गाभ्यां	दुर्गाभिः	फलेन	फलाभ्यां	फलैः
रामाय	रामाभ्यां	रामेभ्यः	दुर्गायै	दुर्गाभ्यां	दुर्गाभ्यः	फलाय	फलाभ्यां	फलेभ्यः
रामात्	रामाभ्यां	रामेभ्यः	दुर्गायाः	दुर्गाभ्यां	दुर्गाभ्यः	फलात्	फलाभ्यां	फलेभ्यः
रामस्य	रामयोः	रामाणां	दुर्गायाः	दुर्गयोः	दुर्गाणां	फलस्य	फलयोः	फलानां
रामे	रामयोः	रामेषु	दुर्गायाम्	दुर्गयोः	दुर्गासु	फले	फलयोः	फलेषु
हे राम	हे रामौ	हे रामाः	हे दुर्गे	हे दुर्गे	हे दुर्गाः	हे फल	हे फले	हेफलानि

Pronoun 7x3 Matrix in 3 genders - No Vocative

तद् –दकारान्तः पुंलिङ्गः He			तद् – दकारान्तः स्त्रीलिङ्गः She			तद् – दकारान्तः नपुंसकलिङ्गः It		
सः	तौ	ते	सा	ते	ताः	तत्	ते	तानि
तं	तौ	तान्	तां	ते	ताः	तत्	ते	तानि
तेन	ताभ्यां	तैः	तया	ताभ्यां	ताभिः	तेन	ताभ्यां	तैः
तस्मै	ताभ्यां	तेभ्यः	तस्यै	ताभ्यां	ताभ्यः	तस्मै	ताभ्यां	तेभ्यः
तस्मात्	ताभ्यां	तेभ्यः	तस्याः	ताभ्यां	ताभ्यः	तस्मात्	ताभ्यां	तेभ्यः
तस्य	तयोः	तेषां	तस्या	तयोः	तासां	तस्य	तयोः	तेषां
तस्मिन्	तयोः	तेषु	तस्यां	तयोः	तासु	तस्मिन्	तयोः	तेषु

Respectful Pronoun (You-Thou) Matrix

भवत् –तकारान्तः पुंलिङ्गः			भवती –ईकारान्तः स्त्रीलिङ्गः			भवत् – तकारान्तः नपुंसक		
भवान्	भवन्तौ	भवन्तः	भवती	भवत्यौ	भवत्यः	भवत्	भवती	भवन्ति
भवन्तं	भवन्तौ	भवतः	भवतीं	भवत्यौ	भवतीः	भवत्	भवती	भवन्ति
भवता	भवद्भ्यां	भवद्भिः	भवत्या	भवतीभ्यां	भवतीभिः	भवता	भवद्भ्यां	भवद्भिः
भवते	भवद्भ्यां	भवद्भ्यः	भवत्यै	भवतीभ्यां	भवतीभ्यः	भवते	भवद्भ्यां	भवद्भ्यः
भवतः	भवद्भ्यां	भवद्भ्यः	भवत्याः	भवतीभ्यां	भवतीभ्यः	भवत्	भवद्भ्यां	भवद्भ्यः
भवतः	भवतोः	भवतां	भवत्याः	भवत्योः	भवतीनां	भवत्	भवतोः	भवतां
भवति	भवतोः	भवत्सु	भवत्यां	भवत्योः	भवतीषु	भवति	भवतोः	भवत्सु
हे भवन्	हे भवन्तौ	हे भवन्तः	हे भवति	हे भवत्यौ	हे भवत्यः	हेभवत्	हेभवती	हेभवन्ति

Vedic Accents

स्वरः Udāta, Anudāta, Svarita, Dirgha Svarita

Accents are marks on the vowels that change the pitch.
Accents are used to highlight that a particular vowel is to be pronounced in a different pitch. A syllable may be pronounced

- from belly, Anudāta, by dropping neck slightly = low pitch
- from heart, Udāta, by keeping a straight face = normal pitch
- from forehead, Svarita, by raising neck slightly = high pitch
- elongating enunciation time, dīrgha Svarita = high to normal

अनुदात्त Anudāta, underline for a vowel, signifies that the pitch is to be lowered, i.e. the sound should come from the belly.

अन् + उदात्तः = अनुदात्तः = ॒

उदात्त Udāta – The normal chant, keeping a straight face. There is no marking for उदात्तः I When Anudāta is followed by Udāta, or vice versa, then a change in pitch will be noticeable.

Svarita – Rise in pitch by lifting the head slightly.

स्वरितः = ॑ a vertical bar on the vowel

Dīrgha Svarita – raising the pitch for a longer duration

दीर्घ स्वरितः = ॥ two vertical bars on the vowel – During chanting, it is noticeable by pronouncing the vowel, giving a short gap, then again pronouncing the vowel.

Vedic Meter or Tune अनुष्टुप् छन्दः

The Bhagavad Gita is written and sung in a definite metre known as the Anushtup Chhanda. So is the Ramayana. This consists of 8 syllables in a quarter, two quarters in a half-verse, and four quarters in a verse.

Chanting Sacred Texts Correctly

Avagraha Ayogavaha Visarga Anusvara

Reading or chanting a Sanskrit text takes into account the appearance of Ayogavaha characters. These characters are uttered in a specific way that is usually taught in a gurukul system.

अवग्रह Avagraha ऽ is not to be chanted, i.e. it is a silent letter.

It signifies that an अ has been dropped due to sandhi.

e.g. Recite प्रथमोऽध्यायः as प्रथमोध्यायः

विसर्ग Visarga ◌ः is pronounced variously, a brief mention

A visarga is pronounced aspirated ह् followed by the sound of the preceding vowel. Thus नमः is to be chanted as नम ह

verse 2.41 बुद्धिः is to be chanted as बुद्धि हि

However, a visarga in close proximity with another letter gets replaced with another letter or even gets dropped. E.g. Visarga when followed by श or च is pronounced as श्

ॐ नमः शिवाय । Chant as ॐ नमश् शिवाय ।

Visarga when followed by स or त is pronounced as स्

पुरुषः सुखदुःखानाम् , भोक्तृत्वे हेतुरुच्यते ॥ १३.२० पुरुषस् सुखदुःखानाम्

Visarga when followed by vowel or soft consonant is dropped or changes to ओ as per context. Consider verse B.Gita 2.16 नासतः विद्यते भावः नाभावः विद्यते सतः । and as it appears in popular editions नासतो विद्यते भावो नाभावो विद्यते सतः ।

Also, a visarga changes to a repha in certain instances.

Ardha Visarga ✕ जिह्वामूलीय / उपधमानीय

Optionally Visarga preceding क, ख is pronounced aspirated ह्

बुद्धियुक्तो जहातीह ,   उभे सुकृतदुष्कृते ।

तस्माद् योगाय युज्यस्व ,   योग✕ कर्मसु कौशलम् ॥ २.५०

But it remains a visarga when the following letter is क्ष (क् ष).

Optionally Visarga preceding प, फ is pronounced aspirated फ

धर्मक्षेत्रे कुरुक्षेत्रे ,   समवेता युयुत्सवः ।

<u>मामका✕ पाण्डवाश्चैव</u> ,   किम् अकुर्वत सञ्जय ॥ १.१

Anusvara ं is pronounced as nasalized म् ।

However Sandhi grammar rules state that Anusvara changes
to a corresponding nasal when followed by a class
consonant, *albeit optionally.*

<u>व्यूढां द्रुपदपुत्रेण</u> ,   तव शिष्येण धीमता ॥ १.३ व्यूढान् द्रुपदपुत्रेण

Others chant an Anusvara as यँ when followed by य ।

तस्मात् सर्वगतं ब्रह्म ,   <u>नित्यं यज्ञे</u> प्रतिष्ठितम् ॥ ३.१५ नित्यँ यज्ञे

In any case it is ok if Anusvara is pronounced as म् ।

Specific Conjuncts

ह्न , ह्ण , ह्म These conjuncts are chanted as नः , णः , मः resp.

पवन✕ पवतामस्मि ,   रामः शस्त्रभृतामहम् ।

झषाणां मकरश्चास्मि ,   <u>स्रोतसामस्मि जाह्नवी</u> ॥ १०.३१ <u>जानःवी</u>

i.e. though it is ह् न , pronunciation is न ह । These letters are
chanted with emphasis on the chest.

स्फोटन Sphotana

When a व्यञ्जन is followed by a क or क्ष there is a natural pause
in reading aloud.

Latin Transliteration Chart

International Alphabet of Sanskrit Transliteration (I.A.S.T.)

a	ā	i	ī	u	ū	ṛ	ṝ	ḷ	
अ	आ	इ	ई	उ	ऊ	ऋ	ॠ	ऌ	
	ा	ि	ी	ु	ू	ृ	ॄ	ॢ	
e	ai	o	au	ṃ	ḥ	Ardha Visarga	oṃ	m̐	
ए	ऐ	ओ	औ	अं	अः	ᳵ	ॐ	ँ	
े	ै	ो	ौ	ं	ः				

Consonants are shown with a vowel 'a= अ' for uttering

ka	क	ca	च	ṭa	ट	ta	त	pa	प
kha	ख	cha	छ	ṭha	ठ	tha	थ	pha	फ
ga	ग	ja	ज	ḍa	ड	da	द	ba	ब
gha	घ	jha	झ	ḍha	ढ	dha	ध	bha	भ
ṅa	ङ	ña	ञ	ṇa	ण	na	न	ma	म
ya	ra	la	va		ḷa	'	.	.	
य	र	ल	व		ळ	S	।	॥	
					Consonant only		halanta		
śa	ṣa	sa	ha		ka	क्अ = क		◌्	
श	ष	स	ह		k	क्			

References

Author-Title-Year-Ed-Publisher

V S Apte-संस्कृत हिन्दी कोश (1890 Ed)-1997-1st -Oriental Book Center, Delhi

Various-भाषा प्रवेशः Vol1 -2015-4th -Samskrita Bharati, New Delhi

Various-प्रवेशः -2015-2nd -Samskrita Bharati, Aksharam, Bangalore

Pushpa Dikshit-शीघ्रबोध—व्याकरणम्-2017-2nd -Pratibha Prakashan, New Delhi

KLV Sastry & Anantarama Sastri – Sabda Manjari 1961– Reprint - 2013 – RS Vadhyar & Sons, Palghat.

https://www.ashtangayoga.info/philosophy/sanskrit-and-devanagari/transliteration-tool/
http://spokensanskrit.org/
http://bhagavadgita.org.in/sanskrit
https://upanishads.org.in/
https://www.sanskritworld.in/index/Sanskrittool
http://ashtadhyayi.com/dhatu/
http://tdil-dc.in/san/skt_gen/generators.html#

Epilogue

The ॐ symbol is created from three parts, namely the "3" shape of अ, the knob from ऊ, and the candrabindu ँ that is used to indicate a nasalized vowel. In other words, Sattva Rajas Tamas & Turiya, or the Trinity that supports creation & Brahman.

सर्वे भवन्तु सुखिनः । सर्वे सन्तु निरामयाः ।

सर्वे भद्राणि पश्यन्तु । मा कश्चिद् दुःख भाग् भवेत् ॥

ॐ शान्तिः शान्तिः शान्तिः ॥

When faith has blossomed in life, Every step is led by the Divine.

Sri Sri Ravi Shankar

Om Namah Shivaya

जय गुरुदेव